Strong Roots

Olia Hercules
Strong Roots

A Ukrainian Family Story of War, Exile and Hope

BLOOMSBURY CIRCUS
LONDON · OXFORD · NEW YORK · NEW DELHI · SYDNEY

BLOOMSBURY CIRCUS
Bloomsbury Publishing Plc
50 Bedford Square, London, WC1B 3DP, UK
Bloomsbury Publishing Ireland Limited,
29 Earlsfort Terrace, Dublin 2, D02 AY28, Ireland

BLOOMSBURY, BLOOMSBURY CIRCUS and the Circus logo are
trademarks of Bloomsbury Publishing Plc

First published in Great Britain 2025

Copyright © Olia Hercules, 2025

Family tree by Veronika Prykhodko

Olia Hercules is identified as the author of this work in accordance with the
Copyright, Designs and Patents Act 1988.

Photographs are from the author's personal collection except Chapter 7,
credit: Universal History Archive/Universal Images Group via Getty Images

Some names and details of individuals have been changed to
preserve their anonymity

All rights reserved. No part of this publication may be: i) reproduced or transmitted
in any form, electronic or mechanical, including photocopying, recording or by
means of any information storage or retrieval system without prior permission in
writing from the publishers; or ii) used or reproduced in any way for the training,
development or operation of artificial intelligence (AI) technologies, including
generative AI technologies. The rights holders expressly reserve this publication
from the text and data mining exception as per Article 4(3) of the Digital Single
Market Directive (EU) 2019/790

A catalogue record for this book is available from the British Library

ISBN: HB: 978-1-5266-6292-7; TPB: 978-1-5266-6294-1;
EBOOK: 978-1-5266-6295-8; EPDF: 978-1-5266-6296-5

2 4 6 8 10 9 7 5 3 1

Typeset by Newgen KnowledgeWorks Pvt. Ltd., Chennai, India
Printed and bound in Great Britain by CPI Group (UK) Ltd, Croydon CR0 4YY

To find out more about our authors and books visit www.bloomsbury.com
and sign up for our newsletters

For product safety related questions contact productsafety@bloomsbury.com

For my big family, ancestors, Ukraine and her people

Contents

Prologue	1
1 Borsch in Italy	13
2 The Great Hush	45
3 Three Thousand Eggs	79
4 The Night Beauty	117
5 The Language of the Nightingales	151
6 A Lesson About Freedom	183
7 Asret	209
8 The World Before the Dam	237
Epilogue	261
Acknowledgements	273

With Sasha in my parents' garden in Kakhovka, 2013

Prologue

A Million Cherry Orchards

I am writing this story without knowing its end: it begins long before I was born and will continue long after I die. I am writing this story to help myself heal and to make you understand. I am writing the story of my ancestors, as well as my own story, which is a microcosm of the story of Ukraine, of its people and of the land itself, where I was born, where I was formed.

22 February 2022

Two days before Russia launched a full-scale invasion on Ukraine, I wrote this message to Putin in my diary: 'You may be rattling your sabre, but we have a million cloaked ghosts, standing at our shoulder, sharpening their scythes, waiting for you. You are right, our "traditions of statehood" have been limited, but despite that we have created a rich culture, a beautiful language and a strong, kind, inclusive and freedom-loving people. These are my ghosts. They may be dead, but their spirit is with me.'

I could not sleep that week, suspended in a smudge state between awake and dreaming. This is when I saw the ghosts. They were cartoonish, monochrome with splashes of red, like in a graphic novel. That night, the wind was bashing against the loft window like an intruder, adding a soundtrack to my hallucination. In my half-dream, the world looked apocalyptic. The spectres stood on the edge of a trench, or a grave, it was hard to tell. There were millions of them. They were skeletal, unrecognisable as humans, but I knew five of them well. They were three of my late grandparents: my mum's parents Liusia, the family matriarch, and Viktor, gentle and quiet, holding in so much; and Vera, my paternal grandmother. There were also the eldest two of Mum's five siblings: her brother Viktor, a font of family knowledge, and sister Zhenia, who was my primary school teacher and the first activist in the family.

Accompanying the ghosts were flashes of family memories. A crowd of us are at the long table under the walnut tree in Liusia's garden, where we would gather for festivities and tell family stories. Sad tales of hunger, deportation, exile, return and silence, interwoven with stories of resilience, abundance, beauty, births and release. Epic narratives worthy of a novel, as well as anecdotes of the quiet everydayness of everyday things, both grounding and inspiring.

I was not asleep. I stretched for my diary and scribbled down the details of what I was seeing, 'Like a chicken with her claw,' as my mum would say, hoping I would be able to decipher the words the next morning. The visions felt formidable and important.

The day that followed that night was particularly tough. Online, I saw a Russian tank in Kyiv driving over and flattening a car, with a person inside it. I found it so impossible to process what was happening in my homeland that I couldn't self-regulate; I had something akin to a panic attack, convinced that the invaders would kill my mum and dad, overtaken by behaviours not my own. I kept shouting, in the kitchen, to my husband Joe, 'I just want to be dead. Please, I just want to be dead.' Eventually, exhausted, I went to bed. I thought of my ghosts, to calm myself. Then, in that semiconscious state, they appeared to me. A little less surreal this time, more human, like how they used to be.

My grandmother Vera came into focus before me. Vera's biggest fear was war. I remember gatherings in her living room, one of the walls tiled and with a red rug hanging on it, a small window opposite, cosy and cave-like, the table heaped with plov, a Central Asian rice dish, and pelmeni dumplings, two of what we called her 'greatest hits'. She would never fail to raise a toast to the absence of war. 'The main thing is that there is no war.'

We would shake our heads at this dismissively; the idea of war was utterly inconceivable. Yet we dutifully repeated the words after her like a mantra and clinked our glasses in approval. Later, back at home, we would remark on Vera's odd little ritual. 'Have you noticed, she always says it like an incantation?'

I fell deeper into somnolence as my ancestors' remains pulsed through the roots of the Earth, seeped through the capillary-like structures of mycelium, travelling from one end of Europe to the other, from underneath the wonky Ukrainian tombstones all the way to my garden table under the old pear tree in London. I find comfort in that, thinking of my connection with my ancestors and the way they live in me and my spaces.

I have always done this. In times of difficulty, I have never prayed to a crusty old man sitting on a cloud, instead I plead with my dead grandmothers in my head. I am sure I'm not the only Ukrainian – or human – who does this.

In 2014, when Russia invaded Eastern Ukraine and the Ukrainian autonomous Republic of Crimea in the south, I was already living in the UK. I'd recently become a lone parent to my one-year-old son, Sasha – named for my brother – and embarked on an uncertain freelance career as a chef and food writer. The invasion really scared me, like I'd never been scared before. Crimea was only 70 kilometres away from where my parents lived, in the Kherson region of Ukraine. They were in Kakhovka, right next to a reservoir that fed indispensable fresh water into the Crimean peninsula. How soon before the Russians moved into my hometown? My anxiety was so debilitating that I realised – if I did not do something – I would struggle to manage my new and terrifying role as a single parent and freelancer. I decided to spend the last of that month's money on my first ever trip to a psychiatrist. She was highly esteemed; it was the most expensive hour of my life.

To begin with, she asked me questions. Simple stuff, such as, 'Do you smoke?' 'How much do you drink?' 'Where were you born?' When she asked me, 'What is your religion, if any?' I blurted out, 'My family!' She raised her eyes at me slowly and then shot them back to the paper she was writing on. It must have sounded so utterly weird and even worrying; possibly cultish. I cringed for days afterwards, berating myself for not explaining further. To me, a non-religious person, my family – including, maybe especially including, my deceased ancestors – has always been the most important, most sacred thing in the world. For Ukrainians, this spiritual devotion to our family and ancestors extends into our home, the temple.

Khata, a Ukrainian word with Persian origins which sounds a little bit like 'hut', roughly translates as 'cottage'. It describes a small house in the countryside. To me, and to many Ukrainians, it evokes the bucolic, almost fantasy-like world of the nineteenth century, but of course the khata still exists today. The original khata was a genius, highly sustainable creation, dreamt up in tandem with nature. It was often made of thatch and mud, especially in central and southern parts of Ukraine, and it was warm in winter and cool in summer. The walls were traditionally limewashed, apart from a black- or red-painted stripe that flowed along the bottom of either the outside or the inside walls. This stripe was a symbolic separation: it divided the ancestral spirits who inhabited the 'roots' of the house from the whitewashed walls above it, which symbolised life in the present. In the past, people would even be buried under the khata porch, endowing the doorway with an important spiritual and ritual significance. The walls of a house, as well as its massive wood-fired masonry oven — called a pich — would be painted with ornate flowers and symbols, talismans that were believed to trap evil spirits and bad luck in their intricate, motley whorls. The pich was seen as an anthropomorphic mother figure, so revered that it was forbidden to swear in her presence. For me, as someone who cooks for a living far away from my homeland, the pich is yet another ghost of home.

There would always be a long bench by the windows in the khata, either embedded in the floor or movable, where women would sit and weave or embroider in winter months. Hand-embroidered — and often hand-woven — linen or hemp cloths called rushnyky would adorn the walls, often draped over icons or, later, photographs. The house would always be spotlessly clean: the intense spiritual and aesthetic commitment of Ukrainians to their homes requires meticulous order.

PROLOGUE

Fifty days after Orthodox Easter, it is believed the spirits of the dead come to life. Not all these are well-intentioned. Some will be your ancestors, but visitors can bring other spirits with them who might be less benign. To ward off the troublesome ghosts, clay, well-rotted sweet manure and hay were mixed by foot and spread across the floor, a special, magical process that involved the young and the old. This was left to dry, firming up into a smooth surface, which was then covered with fragrant dried herbs, grasses and wildflowers (except for cornflowers, known as 'mermaid flowers', which represent more spirits of the dead, usually women who have died young). Sedge grass, wild thyme, lovage, mint, lemon balm, flowering purple basil and wormwood mixed with sweet flag grass would cover the whole floor in a fragrant carpet, so every gentle step inside released heady essential oils, while branches of maple, walnut, birch or oak would be artfully arranged above door frames.

As long as the weather was clement, on the outside of khata walls, underneath the windows or by the fence, flowers bloomed. The twisted stars of periwinkles, towering hollyhocks with their hot-pink Medusa heads, the lion-mane frills of marigolds. And, of course, giant sunflowers, one of many symbols of Ukraine, booming alongside the woven fence. Their heavy heads, the size of cartwheels, bowed down and facing towards the sun, from East to West. Their seeds entwined in neat galactic sequence, not quite black yet, but stripy grey, soft and slightly wet, nature's treat for small children as well as birds.

What I call a 'vegetable patch' was usually a huge field, facing a river to make watering it in the hotter months much easier. Rows of blowsy moss-green cabbages, their thick veins silvered with spider webs, the edges of their tougher outer leaves nibbled by slugs and snails. A row of beetroot, a fanfare of huge, juicy, red-streaked leaves. And then the arresting sight of a pumpkin patch, apocalyptic spheres of swamp-green or orangeade, only good for cattle fodder, too unchallenging to grow, so not as interesting to cook with. ('She gave him a pumpkin,' Ukrainians will say of a woman who has turned down her suitor.) And, of course, here, there and everywhere, tall and spindly dill with its gold-tipped crowns, its royal presence felt in almost every savoury Ukrainian dish. And then the orchard.

A vegetable patch and an orchard are burnt into our country's DNA, indelibly part of our cultural identity. You will probably have heard of Chekhov's Russian Cherry Orchard, but a sour cherry orchard right by a Ukrainian house is a huge part of how we Ukrainians perceive ourselves. The image is crystallised in the public imagination by a poem called 'A Cherry Orchard by the House' by Taras Shevchenko, poet and artist and forger of Ukrainian identity. (In 1847 he was exiled to the Urals for ten years, because he was part of the Kyrylo-Mefodiiv Brotherhood and his poetry was deemed 'revolutionary'.) The poem conjures up images

PROLOGUE

of a family dinner being prepared, the orchard itself wrapped in the comforting hum of bees, the chattering of young girls. At night, by the light of the evening star, nightingales sing. This is the idyllic essence of Ukraine, the place we all go in our heads when things feel tough.

I think of my mother's house. The house I grew up in only had three trees: the fast-growing walnut tree by the outside toilet and two cherry trees at the front, one planted for my brother and one for me. I always resented that Sasha's tree was healthy and sprightly, but mine, only a couple of metres away, was forever ill, its leaves curled in on themselves and its cherries filled with worms. Later, we moved into something bigger, where Mum could at last plant an orchard of her own.

I have a series of snapshots in my head where I walk through my mum's orchard. The boozy windfall plums and unripe quinces with their felt cheeks. Leafy cherry trees, the fruit all gone, gobbled up by us and by the birds, and trees with ripening white and flat peaches. Other trees bearing hard little green apples. When my son Sasha was little, we would visit every September. As I walked round the garden, I'd find that most of the apples hanging on the lower branches bore his teethmarks.

In that spring of 2014, when Russian soldiers in green uniforms claimed a huge swathe of Ukrainian territory in Crimea next door to where I was born, I woke up one night, as I did most nights, cold sweat making my sheets wet. I remember reaching over Sasha's star-shaped body, asleep next to me, to grab my phone from the bedside table, overloaded as it was with glasses of water, food magazines, children's books and nose sprays. It was 3 a.m. I swiped my thumb over and over again, refreshing the news search page or checking my messages. Have they gone further, crossed into Kherson? Are they approaching the North Crimean canal and the dam, a mere twenty minutes away from my family?

Suddenly, all my grandparents' stories came crashing down on me like the heavy lid of a tomb. The intergenerational soup of trauma was now heavily seasoned with the salt of current events, events that were happening to me. Salt makes all the other flavours come out in food, and it turned my family's history — the stories I'd been told throughout my life — from abstract myths, gothic fairytales, into something tangible. I did not want to pass on the weight of this trauma to my own child, but I firmly, unwaveringly wanted — and still want — Sasha to feel Ukrainian.

At the time, though, I wasn't ready to process my family's story, or that of my home country. There was still so much to unpack surrounding my understanding of Ukraine's history, my own sense of identity and what it means to be Ukrainian. But since the big war started, in February 2022, I finally feel ready. So many things have become crystal clear. Being Ukrainian is about moving beyond generational trauma. It's about courage and stoicism and it's about our innate love of

PROLOGUE

freedom. It is also about a culture of kindness, tolerance and connection, in opposition to the violence, bigotry and emotional dissonance we have often faced. Now, I want to tell my story, to sew a small stitch in the vast, rich and colourful embroidery of all Ukrainian lives, whether they be within Ukraine, in exile, or part of the 20-million-strong diaspora.

Call this book a complicated grief response, if you like.

Olga and Petro, Zaporizhzhia, 1979

I

Borsch in Italy

It's a Monday in April 2022. I'm waiting for my parents to arrive in Northern Italy. From where I'm standing, I can look down the hill and see Lago Maggiore… and it is indeed huge. It looks not unlike the Dnipro River back home in South Ukraine. They fascinate me, these inland bodies of fresh water that feel oversized and give you the impression that you are standing on the edge of the sea. I am in my cousin Ihor's new holiday home. It is called Villa d'Angelo, and the previous owners took the name a bit too literally. It is covered in angels, inside and out. Ihor is my mum's nephew, her late sister Zhenia's son. Because there was a big age gap between Zhenia and Mum, Ihor is actually only six years younger than Mum, nearing his sixtieth birthday. Like his father, Sasha, Ihor was a successful trauma surgeon in Ukraine. Then, about fifteen years ago, he emigrated to Germany, worked hard, learned the language, passed numerous exams and finally set up his own clinic.

This is not the first time I have visited this house. We came last year, in 2021, straight after Ihor bought it. Mum, me, Ihor's sister Iryna and her children, Ihor and his partner and their two fluffy dogs all arrived in October. It was a four-day weekend, after a long Covid break, and we couldn't get enough of each other. We sat in the autumnal garden, walked by the shores of the lake, took a trip to Bergamo, bought a kilo of wild mushrooms, made egg noodles by hand, celebrated the new house and discussed what needed to be done to renovate it. The ceilings had beautiful airy frescoes, all frothy cerulean blue. But there was ugly wallpaper, wooden panelling and a lot of huge plastic plants. Nevertheless, we could imagine: the walls would be stripped and painted an old white, the heavy damask curtains swapped for light linen and we would all be able to meet here – this time aesthetically satisfied – in the springtime.

It is now that spring. But instead of a crowd of relatives and fluffy dogs, it is just me, waiting for my parents, who are fleeing their home in Ukraine. I am taking a break after my journey from London via Milan and I am reading a memoir, a humorous book, which is what I sorely need. On the endnotes of the book, there is a shopping list I'd scribbled earlier: olive oil, tonic water, butter, bread, eggs, mortadella for Dad, beer, beetroot, cabbage, beans, onions, carrots, dill (with a double underscore for emphasis), meat (for borsch and ragu), tomato passata, garlic, cheese. To the right of the list, I have scrawled, 'I want to cook!'

For months now, I have not been able to cook. Even eating has been difficult. A friend of a friend, Amy, sent me medicinal Chinese broth every single week in the post. It was the thing that saved me, as I could only manage to drink, not chew.

Losing the ability and desire to cook felt strange, like losing a part of myself. Before, whenever I felt daily stress, or a hint of depression approaching, I would cook. Something bread-related, usually. The soft dough under the cushion of my palm, its stickiness, its comforting sweet-sour aroma, the repetitive movements... the ultimate act of mindfulness. Kneading dough is a sensory repetition that forces you to observe the moment, to let go of the insistent buzz of anxiety. It is not only work for me, a quotidian family chore, it is an act of self-care. I must have felt that cooking was therapy in my early twenties, subconsciously, as self-care wasn't in our vocabulary twenty years ago.

I grew up among incredible cooks, but in Ukraine you don't — or at least we didn't — cook at your mother's side. The adults were busy, you were not to get in the way, but I must have absorbed a lot of it by osmosis. Suddenly, when I turned twenty, I wanted to cook. Very quickly, it became an obsession. Normally chaotic, anxious, messy, clumsy, I turned into someone else when I cooked. I often imagined myself like a drawing;

a human body, yes, but my head was an explosion of pixels, distorted, springing every which way. When I cooked, I would become composed, focused and happy. I loved this feeling. And it made me feel closer to the family I was missing.

I came to the UK when I was eighteen, to study at university, and it was exciting to be independent, especially for the first year. But then I started missing Mum, Dad, my brother Sasha and my huge extended family. In Ukraine, we do not really have a term equivalent to 'extended', it is just family. Through cooking, I could connect to them again, and on a deeper level.

The familiar smells, the sounds of chopping and stirring and the buzz of serving my food to my first husband and friends made the addiction to cooking stronger and stronger. I was chasing the feeling that cooking gave me, like it was a drug, until I decided to turn it into my profession. The idea was – and I often said it – that even if I had to work for peanuts in a restaurant for the rest of my life, I could be happy just chopping. Chopping for my remaining years would give me what I was missing. It would hold my head together, those tiny little pixels forming a completed picture through the sense-enveloping, repetitive actions of my hands. Only recently, though, have I pieced all this together. Before, I thought of it as an unexplained compulsion. Just like my paternal grandmother, Vera.

Dad often reprimanded Vera for cooking so many dishes when we visited. Her extendable table would be crammed with serving dishes of braised chicken and mash, sliced tomatoes and cucumbers in the summer or their pickled versions in winter, dumplings, Uzbek plov and beshbarmak meat and noodles, a plastic bottle each of homemade wine and grape juice. He used to say, 'Mama, stop working yourself to death! We should be more European now.' (By that, I think he meant 'modern'.) 'Just cook one main dish and one salad!' She resisted. Dad's proposed concept of restrained cooking and feeding was alien to her. Now, I realise all that movement and focus was good for Vera, especially as she got older. She wasn't working herself to death, she was cooking herself to life.

On 24 February 2022, everything changed. Ukraine was invaded by Russia and Kherson, my home region, was occupied. We should have known it was coming. It's mad to think of it only now, but even though the Russians had been occupying neighbouring Crimea since 2014, it had never felt as though we were bordering Russia. We lived in Ukraine and in our minds it felt untouchable, unchangeable. Yet soon after Russia's invasion of Crimea, the whitewashed fences in our area were painted in the blue and yellow of the Ukrainian flag: a signal, a confirmation of unity within the community. As things settled and calmed, we were lulled into a feeling of safety. Perhaps we should have known better, realised that one day trouble would come to us too. And maybe we should have prepared, maybe my parents should have been ready.

When the unimaginable happened in 2022, I could not function normally. I could not eat. Needless to say, I could not cook either. In fact, cooking suddenly felt painful. Instead of healing me as it always had before, it hurt. The act of cooking was interwoven so tightly with my family and my homeland that even the mundane act of chopping through a cabbage made me burst into tears. Cooking also felt like frivolity. How can I cook while my brother is running with a gun in a forest, defending Kyiv, and my mum and dad are living under occupation? Any hint of pleasure felt like a betrayal. And cooking, one of the biggest pleasures in my life, felt like the biggest betrayal. It just did not feel right, and sometimes I feared I might have lost my superpower forever.

In the first few weeks of March, Mum and Dad were stoic and brave, travelling into the centre of town to protest every day. It was their home; they said they were not going to leave unless missiles fell on their heads. But such public protest quickly became impossible. There was shooting and the sound of grenades constantly. Local government officials, journalists, activists started to go missing. First the new occupier-installed mayor of the town phoned my dad. 'We need the keys to your B&B business.' Dad said it was out of the question. Then, the next day, a Russian called. 'We know your son is in the territorial army. Tell him to put down his arms or else.'

Dad said it was too dangerous to leave. He said he was responsible for his thirty-five employees at the farming equipment plant – and their livelihoods, as well as for all the animals at home: their dogs, ducks and chickens.

When internet and mobile connections cease and there is no communication with the outside world, it is easier to commit crimes, as well as to cover them up. And in the days after the massacre at Bucha was revealed to the world, it became harder and harder to keep in touch with anyone in the Kherson region. I was in the kitchen when I managed to video-call my parents, after forty-eight hours of agonised waiting. The roaming on their phones was disappearing, a toe-curling sign of impending danger. I finally lost it. 'You are responsible for me!' I screamed to my dad when I got through. 'For your grandchildren. What will happen to us? How will Sasha cope? How will Joe? I will not be able to live, Papa. PLEASE LEAVE.' If in that moment I had not been feeling so deeply shocked and traumatised, you could have called me manipulative. I now believe it was an essential, life-saving manipulation. My mum came on the line and tried to calm me down. We would speak again tomorrow.

That night, I watched a Zoom seminar given by a journalist from Kakhovka, Oleh Baturin, who had been kidnapped and, thankfully, released. He relayed the secrets of his recent successful evacuation. I noted the important details: no tinted car windows (less likely to be shot at); do not hide anything, such as money or jewellery, be transparent. Make sure you have cigarettes and canned food; Russian soldiers, especially the young ones, are hungry and will ask for food and cigarettes.

Baturin pleaded with everybody on the call who remained in the region to leave now, while the Russians at checkpoints were still mostly young and clueless. He warned that, soon, the region would be teeming with FSB officers clutching special blacklists. These are lists of the names of people who are destined for 'filtration camps' – interrogation and detention centres – where Russians determine how Ukrainian their captive appears to be. If you are deemed, or found out, to be 'too Ukrainian', you will be sent to Russia, sometimes as far as Vladivostok by the border with North Korea.

I wrote pages and pages of evacuation notes, took map route screenshots and sent them all to my parents, extended family and friends who were still in Kakhovka and thought it was impossible (or too risky) to leave. Make sure to go in a convoy of at least three cars. If you spot any FSB officers (the scariest of them all), pretend to be naïve, even a bit dim. I advised method acting throughout the whole trip. 'I expect nothing but an Oscar, especially from you, Mum. Control your eye rolls and do not let them see you narrow your eyes in disgust when they talk to you!'

The next day, my parents finally conceded. I promised my dad that I would help raise money to support his and Mum's employees. I convinced my Uncle Slava, Aunt Liuda and cousin Aliona, her husband and her kids to join them. And even my most patriotic, unwavering friend and baker Katrya Kaluzhna and her carpenter husband Sasha. My uncle and family left on

Wednesday. My parents on Thursday. Katrya with her husband and friends on Friday.

On Wednesday night I had a dream; at first, in my sleep, I braced myself for another night terror. My body felt paralysed, but I understood it was a dream and I was observing myself from above. I was lying on my side, one of my arms stretched straight and upwards, my head turned up, observing my hand. A large black spider, bigger than a tarantula, was circling around my hand. I felt fear, but I could not move. Then I managed to turn the palm of my hand so it was facing upwards. The spider stopped circling, crawled into my palm and immediately became smaller, more compact, as if it was curling itself up for a rest... and I felt calm. The next morning, my parents broke through nineteen Russian checkpoints and successfully left my native, now Russian-occupied Ukraine.

I bought a flight to Milan as soon as they managed to cross the border between occupied Kherson into the still-free Mykolayiv region.

The Villa d'Angelo greets me, a musty but light ochre yellow, with its big terrace and stone-white balustrades framed by palm trees and pampas grass. I need to make Mum and Dad feel at home, so I decide to make borsch. My parents would step into a house of familiar smells: fried onions and grated carrots, beetroot, chicken fat, freshly cut dill... or, at the very least, parsley. There would also be soothing murmurs from the bubbling and gentle susurration at the stove. They would feel the comforting dampness of a kitchen where a huge pot of borsch has been cooking for hours, steaming up the walls, dripping down the windows. I would scour the garden, or a nearby dirt track, and look for flowers to put into the little vase. Small signals that would tell them: 'You are safe, I am here, we can still have borsch and drinks and flowers, and as long as we can sit around a table together and see and feel those things together, it cannot be the end.'

Back in March and early April 2022, I sent a message to my parents every single morning: Yak vy? ('How are you?') If they replied, it was a fairly good day. If my phone remained silent, it was not. I would try again the following day. And then, one morning, a very hopeful answer came from my mum: 'Today we made borsch, and it nourished us and made us feel stronger. I really feel like it's an element of our DNA.' There was a borsch-related and courage-inducing story circling online at the beginning of the big war (though I still don't know if it was true), about Ukrainian soldiers planting beetroot and onion seeds in trenches. It does feel like fiction now, a unifying myth perhaps, but even if someone invented it to raise morale, it is a signifier of what is important to us, what kind of people Ukrainians are. I imagined the seedlings growing at the upper edge of the trench. Could it even be possible? Wouldn't it be too loud for baby plants to want to grow? The constant shelling, the soldiers moving, unsettling that soil. But the idea was powerful; I believed the story at the time and it did give me strength.

A story which is most definitely true – I saw reportage of it on the Ukrainian news – is that groups of volunteers all over the country started making 'instant borsch' to be sent to the front lines. I watched women chop half a tonne of vegetables a day, thinly sliced cabbage, cooked squares of potato, grated carrots and beetroot, all sprinkled into multi-layered dehydrators. The women said proudly, 'We come from Kherson. We want to help. Every ingredient in our instant borsch packets is organic. Look at all these vegetables. The boys do not have time to cook borsch for two hours in the trenches. But they can pour hot water over our dried borsch mix and, within fifteen minutes, they have something nutritious and tasty!'

I remember Mum telling me about her first experience of cooking at the age of seven. The story was told with a sense of wonder and surprise, rather than any pride, any sense of 'look at me, I was already cooking at such a young age'. It sounded like an adventure, a foray into independence, a world of performing adult tasks. Her mother, Liusia, a 'blood-and-milk' type normally full of health and raw energy, was ill with flu and could not get out of bed. The bed was made from metal in the form of a metallic net, stretched from pole to pole. This meant that, if you got into the bed, it caved in, almost like a hammock. It was fine for one person, but if Mum crawled in to lie with her mother in the middle of the night, woken by a nightmare, she would roll right on top of her. There were no mattresses, but thick and heavy goose-down duvets.

Liusia's bed was underneath a huge window that, in the late 1950s, had looked out into the garden. By the early 1960s it was a portal to the new kitchen, which had been built as an annexe attached to the outside wall of the house. This meant that Liusia, her voice as hoarse as coals, could direct my seven-year-old Mum through making borsch via the massive window. The new kitchen was small, a blueish-white cocoon of uneven limewashed walls. Most of the place was taken up by the plyta, a handmade brick oven, also whitewashed, with a cast-iron plate with two large rings, and then a different kind of an oven, which did not get hot enough to bake bread in but was good for making the baked milk yogurt called ryazhanka. There was no gas at that time, so in summer they cooked on a kerosene hotplate, but in winter they used this rough Aga-style plyta, which was fed wood and coals and repaid that kindness by providing enough heat to cook, as well as warming the adjacent bedroom. In went paper and light pieces of wood, then a match, then coals. On top of the cast-iron rings, a chipped white enamel teapot rested; it almost never left its post during the winter. It was full of red berries – rose hips and haws – a wintertime elixir, lending the kitchen a perpetual aroma of sour, herby plums.

Mum's story felt like a fairytale to me. I pictured her climbing up on the stout wooden stool, picking up the big rugged knife with its beaten-up handle and chopping for the first time, slowly, pieces of vegetables pinging from the blunt blade all over the wooden floor. But it was OK, Liusia was too ill to care. Mum heaved the big empty aluminium pot on to the ring, filled a jug of water from the tap and emptied it into the pot at least ten times, until there was enough. A whole bird, a skinny chicken, its skin dry and bumpy, head still on, lowered in the pot by the legs, leathery clawed feet sticking out until it had boiled enough to fully submerge. Mum does not remember how that first borsch came out. It was all about the process, the responsibility, the idea that she was grown up and taking on the role of carer for the first time. She also fed herself, and it felt good.

Only last week, Mum told me about a dream she'd had. In the thirty years since her father died, she had only dreamt about him once until last week. In the dream, she was a child. Her father Viktor came into the room, he was hungry. Mum had made borsch. She poured the thick broth into his bowl, the ladle catching two large pieces of oxtail. She thinks to herself that they are the best bits, and she wants them for herself. She feels a childlike sense of accomplishment in this selfless act of sharing. Then suddenly she is in the present, a mother. She is looking at her son Sasha and his spine is on fire. A neat strip of flames, like a burning row of pine trees in a forest, is glowing all along his vertebrae. She puts out the fire with a bowl of cold borsch, thick and gelatinous from beef collagen.

I arrive at the villa at 9:30 in the morning and by 10, I am off again. I have six hours to shop and cook and tidy up, just enough time, so long as nothing goes wrong. I walk down the hill to the supermarket with a spring in my step. The April air is cool on my face, but the late morning sun feels warm on my shoulders, warm like a cat's belly. I feel something close to euphoria, almost manic. They got out! I don't think I have ever felt a relief as profound as this, except perhaps after giving birth. It is how I would imagine feeling when doctors give you a terrible diagnosis… but then quickly realise they have made a mistake. The blissful anticipation of seeing my parents, watching them eat, being able to squeeze their hands and hear their voices mingles with the sunshine and birdsong around me. It propels me forward to almost run down the hill, arms swinging, childlike. I know their story is going to be difficult for them to tell and for me to hear and I know there will be tears, but at least we will have a familiar, warm bowl of soup to eat and a glass of beer to sip slowly, giving us a chance to pause, to reshuffle thoughts, words and emotions.

The supermarket looks generic and soulless and my heart drops at the sight. The possibility of not finding any beetroot, which Italians don't use much, suddenly strikes me as I approach the plastic glow of the shop's entrance and the scaffolding around it. I step inside and gasp, as any avid cook would: do not judge a shop by its cover! Immediately I spot agretti, or monk's beard, a wild marsh-dwelling weed, then I see bitter-leafed puntarelle, a few types of artichokes, all niche ingredients only found in specialist shops in London. In another life, I would have squealed at this seasonal cornucopia, a food lover's dream. But on this occasion, I frantically move my eyes from one colourful patch of greengrocery to another, searching for a glimpse of earthy purple or dark muddy pink. No fresh beetroot. I remind myself to breathe: it is not the end of the world if borsch does not happen.

Calmly, I walk to the fridge and spot vacuum-packed boiled beetroot, the last on the shelf. There is no dill in sight, but there is parsley, which will do. I need a good chicken. A good chicken which has had a long and active life. It needs to be old and wiry, the energy of its movement and years of its age transferred into flavour. This type of bird is what makes the borsch sing. I scan the butcher counter, from one fat bird to another, until I see her: pollo per brodo, a boiling chicken, corn-yellow and dinosauric, full of flavour no doubt, just like at home. Having covered the deal-breaking essentials, I fill my basket with white onions and carrots, a young head of cabbage and – hooray! – panna acida (sour cream). I also throw in some olives and pickled anchovies, eggs, flour, minced meat, cheese. I cannot resist asparagus or the monk's beard, as I am sure my parents have never tried it. I grab a six-pack of beer, too.

'I want to cook!' It's time to start. The chicken's skin is torched with a dodgy lighter, to get rid of the stubbly roots of feathers on the legs and wing tips. It creates a scent that teleports me to my childhood. Chickens, ducks, even geese, held over the hob's flame, turned this way and that. It's a smell both similar and entangled with the scent of an extinguished match: sulphuric, warm, animal. I never have to do this in the UK, as the birds I buy are meticulously plucked. For the first time, I wonder how. Do they scald the carcasses in hot water? Do they use industrial plucking machines? I've never thought of this before. Why did my mum have to singe the birds and I never do?

The bottle of tomato passata is so good that there is no need for that pinch of sugar. I chop the squeaky cabbage, young and porous rather than tightly packed, and I do not cry this time. The soggy pre-boiled beetroot is not good enough. In our family, a firm, raw root — all pinks and whites — would be cut into almost perfect matchsticks and boiled together with the meat in plenty of water, dyeing it a muddy yellow. This beetroot makes the stock turn brownish-purple. After an hour, I skim some fat off the surface and pour it into a frying pan. The onions are diced and the carrots roughly grated and I fry them both in the skimmed chicken fat. The onions and carrots are to be cooked gently, all the sugars drawn out to sweeten the earthy stock. The sound of the vegetables frying is both comforting and useful, for as soon as the noise quietens, I know that they have absorbed the tasty fat and that most of their water has been released and has evaporated, so now they could burn.

It was my maternal grandmother Liusia who taught us to listen to our cooking. Whenever she made nudli, a dish of pork stew covered in huge swirly dumplings, she would say, 'Wait until you hear enough spirit in it,' by which she meant it needed to be on a hard boil, 'then add the dumplings.' No wonder the act of cooking has such power over so many of us: it forces us to stay truly in the moment, a trope of every meditation practice from art to prayer. To be a good cook, you need to see, smell, taste and hear. And there is no better way to feel alive.

The onions and carrots, now soft, sweet and frazzled at the edges, are scraped into the stock with a couple of satisfying plops. I don't peel the potatoes, a recent habit and unorthodox for borsch-making. I cube and drop them in, to be cooked until a knife goes in as easily as if they were butter. In go the beans, not red kidney, but a tin of borlotti, which will do nicely. The sliced red pepper and the cabbage are prepped and set aside to be added strictly at the last minute, to cook very briefly, retaining their freshness and a little texture. This, our borsch, has to be thick with vegetables. To test it, stick a wooden spoon in its centre. If it stands proud, my mother would be too.

I want to cook so much that I cannot stop. I crack six eggs into a bowl, one for every 100 grams of flour. The pasta dough is bright yellow – a plasticine sun – and there is a lot of it, but it will keep. I have to leave in two days, but my parents will stay here indefinitely. For the sauce, I dice onions, carrots and celery, add salt and simmer them in lots of green-tinged olive oil. I add minced meat, crank up the heat and fry it off, passata goes in... and then I regret not buying wine. More salt, a generous crackle from the pepper grinder and a whole bushy sprig of basil. The dough has by now rested, so I roll bits of it out into thin sheets, toss flour on it and fold it up, then slice this flattened scroll across into thin noodles. I could have just bought pasta, but the gates are now open wide and I can't stop.

In order to feel like I'm not having too much of a relaxing time while cooking, I listen to a Ukrainian podcast, presented by two psychiatrists. The topic is 'A wartime episode: what are we going through now?' They talk about trauma and touch on the feeling of survivor's guilt. It's my introduction to the concept, but it describes perfectly what I am already feeling. They also talk of different types of trauma, of those who experience it from the epicentre of the action (my parents), to those who experience it vicariously, in our modern age, through screens (that would be me). They talk about how to tackle the gamut of feelings that most of us are experiencing: a cauldron of anger, guilt, shame and hatred. How to survive the gaslighting employed against us by the enemy? I know that these two specialists are not just talking theoretically from a neutral or even indifferent psychologist's couch. They have been through it. Both were in Kyiv when the war started; now, they are in relative safety, in Western Ukraine.

Soon enough, the kitchen is filled with steam, hope and familiar, comforting smells. It is time to forage for more beauty. The garden is big and wild, and, like the house, has the potential to be grand. The palm trees, a local status symbol, are taller than the orange roof. There is an ancient persimmon tree and a gnarled kiwi tree, still bare, twisting its branches around the chipped white bones of the wrought-iron gazebo. Two giant tufts of pampas grass tower over my head and are beautiful. I gently snap off two of its rodded plumes. I pick some dandelions, daisies, buttercups and a single rose that survived February and March, just like we did. They go into a small crystal vase; garlic, lemons and white onion nestled into a ruffled blue bowl beside them. Then I set out the essential chilled beers, olives, a cold seafood salad and anchovies from the deli counter, their crystal bowls throwing long shadows over the warm, dusk-lit table. The massive pot of borsch is too big really for the three of us and is almost spilling over the edge, the chicken's ankles sticking out daftly. I overdid it in my cooking fervour.

Then Mum phones, they are five minutes away. I chuck the cabbage into the borsch and rush out. I stand in the middle of the kinked, steep road, stopping the upcoming cars like a strict traffic warden to help my dad manoeuvre into the garage.

Dad's beard is completely white. He looks exhausted, his eyelids are heavier than normal and two puffy bags hang beneath his eyes. His head and hands shake more than usual. A five-day car trip... it would exhaust you even if you weren't fleeing a war. I don't know how my mum does it, but on the surface, she looks as good as always; her short hair, black in the past, now white and dyed a pinkish blonde for ease, is perfect. She has lipstick on, as always. Later, she shows me her wartime manicure; the red shellac has grown out halfway up her nails. I tried to make an effort too, for her sake, changing from a flour-covered green holey jumper to a striped t-shirt and clean, black dungarees. No manicure for me for many years now. I know that, secretly, my parents think I am a slob, but in the last couple of years they have accepted that I will be forever make-up-less and scruffy, with my visibly mended socks and beaten-up worker's boots. We are hugging, fussing. I grab the big bag. Dad takes it from me and gives me a smaller one. We hug again, and suddenly I feel just how thin my mum is, compared to the last time we embraced in January.

I expected to see more bags. Actually, I expected to see my parents' car filled to the brim, in my imagination even with furniture, like a couple who are moving house. But they are not moving house. They are fleeing. Everything was done in haste and with emotions that are very hard to try and understand. What would it feel like to have to leave your home suddenly? What would you take?

The house they left behind had been our home since 1997, when I was thirteen: a house on the bank of

Dnipro reservoir, with a huge amount of space around it. Dad immediately dug out a massive pond (more like a small lake!) and filled it with lily pads and fish. We all protested at first, exclaiming that we wanted a swimming pool, but he put his foot down with a decisive 'I want a pond!' The pond resembled the local floodplains: an ancient willow and an oak towered over the edges and reeds grew by its side. Before long, storks and kingfishers came to feed and the pond was inhabited by a hundred frogs. Dad filled it with carp and sturgeon.

He hired a local handyman who dabbled in sculpture and made fairytale-like figures out of cement: a frog lying by the water, a webbed hand under its head, eyes closed. A ram's head protruded out of a fence. A quirky bridge. A goat's head above the French doors in the basement. A whole 4-metre cement tree (!) with a gaping mouth and eyes and a well inside. Mum and I exchanged wide-eyed looks and she quietly ordered some ivy.

They planted an orchard of fifteen trees. Mum insisted on creating the vegetable patch, despite my dad's protestations: 'Too backward! They have supermarkets in Ukraine now, don't you know?' She filled the patch with tomatoes, cucumbers, peppers, five types of basil (purple, vanilla, cinnamon, regular and lemon varieties), dill, coriander, parsley… the essentials. In later years, she planted strawberries and a small lavender grove.

And they built a large summer kitchen, our family's gathering space. We called it 'Mum's HQ'. It was a guest house by night and a place to lunch and relax with my big family during the day, and it was Mum's sanctuary when guests were absent. She spent both summers and winters there. In winter, next to the cosy wood burner, she would embroider or knit, watching movies on her iPad while she stitched. Just a few steps away from this magical outbuilding, Dad planted pine and fir trees. A pine-tree dell, forever covered with a soft carpet of brown needles. He also planted grapevines by the entrance to the house, simply because he wanted to arrive home from work, park his car and pick some grapes before going indoors. A sweet little fantasy, easy to realise. The grapes were sticky, aromatic and so jealously coveted by the wasps that the bunches had to be wrapped in gauze pouches each August.

It was my parents' home to retire in, to grow weathered in, alongside the creased riverbank that stretched just below.

My husband Joe, my son Sasha and I would stay in the summer kitchen whenever we visited. We would move the wide handmade sofas together and turn them into a bed at night. The last time I was there in August 2021 – though I didn't know it would be the last time – was the first trip our one-year-old Wilfred had made to Ukraine. I wrote in my diary: 'It is evening and the day has been sticky hot, close to 37°C. Wilf is snoring quietly behind a thick jacquard curtain separating "the bedroom" from the kitchen. I am using my clip-on book light as a little table lamp. There is a warm, peach-coloured reflection of me and my diary in a whisky glass filled with Uncle Misha's homemade Isabella wine. Margarita Liberaki's *Three Summers* is nestled in the corner of the upcycled Singer sewing machine side table that I am using as a desk.

'I can't make out whether it's mosquitoes or little flies keeping me company. I want to make sure they are mosquitoes before I squash them. Their bites are so vicious. There is lightning in the electric-blue sky but no thunder yet. The Dnipro River – with its crayfish, zander, carp and catfish – is rustling beneath us, almost as loud as the sea. In winter, the water can get agitated. There is a stray wild grapevine that is trembling, a little lock freed from the tight plait of the canopy. My senses sharpened by the atmosphere of the approaching summer storm, I keep jumping, thinking it's a snake or a monkey's tail. Mum's oleander is a tall beast. It's my favourite. Wildly poisonous leaves, it turns out. But how beautiful, with that white-pink blossom.

'Thunder is scratching its belly now against the silhouette of the scraggly top edge of the factory buildings peeping just above our fence. This is Ukraine, I think. So much natural beauty on one side, and an industrial behemoth on another. I wonder if I need to put the mosquito repellent on (called Kysh-Komar!, 'Mosquito, Be Gone!') or if the wind will blow them all away. I feel the same about the hovering Russian forces by our frontiers.

'Earlier this evening, I was watching Wilfred's dusk-lit puff of curls. It is time. The heavy Taurida heat subsides; we can come out from the awning's leafy shade and explore. As always, we begin at the kitchen door, down a slender stone path, the river languid and waiting to be dressed in the blush robes of the setting sun. First come the decorative Japanese quince trees with tiny little quinces, then the "real" quince trees. We gently stroke the fuzzy green fruit, taking turns. The quinces have another two months to go. I carry Wilf into Mum's orchard and point at the different trees and shrubs and flowers. I tell him when his older brother was his age he used to secretly run from tree to tree and bite into the low-hanging apples, little toothmarks discovered on each fruit still hanging on the trees, to our amusement and delight. The apples too are still green, it's been a while since we tasted them. The floor is strewn with windfall plums. They are sweet and fizzing. The orchard smells of alcohol and the maenads of the insect world, the wasps, are busy filling up their energy tanks with plummy sugar.

'The cherries are long gone. I miss the fresh cherries, but Mum always thoughtfully freezes bags of the sour ones, so she can stone and wrap them in circles of delicate, thin dough. Varenyky: the dumplings of all seasons and all regions of Ukraine. From kraut and mushrooms to fresh fruit, a shapeshifter dish of our childhood. Here it is savoury, and here it is sweet, filled with berries and drenched in butter, sour cream and sugar.

'We shuffle towards the walnut tree. The tree is by the lavender and pine corner. My mum put a little bench there, as you get the best peek at the river from that spot, not obstructed by the sylph-like, ashen poplars. A dense rug of brown pine needles lies underneath our bare feet; I grab them with my toes to lift and drop them. I pluck a few walnuts from the trees and we sit on the bench. I bash at the nut's tight, mantis-green armour. As soon as the walnut splits, the crumbly skin smells both sweet and saline: so familiar, but not familiar like the walnuts of my childhood smelled. This is new-familiar. I realise it smells like a sea urchin; my brain buzzes from such a niche connection. I peel off the skin to get to the mild and milky kernel, making sure to also scrape off the bitter, slippery membrane. We put the kernels into our mouths and they feel sweet, the texture crumbly and fragile.

'We move on and pick a couple of small, starburst raspberries, but most of them are not yet at their best. And I point towards a Cornelian cherry, perfectly ripe, but bitter and astringent from its tannins, like quince, which people say are best when cooked slowly, when their tough fibres soften into a mush. But there is also pleasure in eating both of these fruits raw, as I did with quince – knowing no different – as a child. I bite a little bit of the Cornelian cherry and offer it to Wilf.

'Our foraging complete, we stop and peer inside a pale hibiscus. Within it lies an illusion of a small flower nestled inside a big flower. The long sticky pistil is topped with lime-coloured pollen. Some of it falls inside the concave of the petals and quivers, moved by the gentlest of breezes. We sniff, or rather I sniff in and Wilf huffs out, but the pleasure is all visual. It is Mum's roses that we need for olfactory pleasures. We walk past the arch snake-wrapped by a tecoma, with its carmine trumpets, tooting songs of bees in different directions. This is where the big orb spider lives, its abdomen a geometric wonder. We say: "Pryvit, pavuk" ("Hello spider"). The roses stand together: a gang, behind a low wattle fence. They are all colours, butter-yellow and magenta, velvet-black and Dutch orange and, my favourite, puppy-belly pink and smelling like almond cake. Next is the bush of giant hibiscus, more precisely Hibiscus syriacus "Pink Giant". What a name! The flowers are fuchsia, almost garish – "Stick your eye out", as Dad would say. They are the size of my head. They are ridiculous. I tell Wilf they are summoning the bees with their round heads. We shift towards and behind the gazebo, close to the creeping rose bush and chives that must have self-seeded and pierced through the paving stones.

'I keep turning my head to the Dnipro River. Now there are quick, ruffled ripples, now it is still like a sheet of glass.'

I think it's this garden that my parents loved the most about their home.

I help Mum and Dad into the ugly living room with the beautiful ceilings. I take a photo of their bags. I don't know why I do that. The incredulity of it, I guess. One, two, three. Three suitcases, two of them little, and some rucksacks. How can this be? Where is their stuff? Dad wants a beer immediately and I don't blame him. I tend to the borsch; the cabbage is overcooked, but I ignore that for now. Mum takes a shower, she needs to wash the past five days off before she settles in for dinner and more hugs. The sun is now hidden behind the mountains, it is close to 6 p.m. and it's the witching hour, the gloaming. It feels almost magical, or maybe I just feel like a child again.

We sit around the table while the light gets deeper, a butterscotch yellow picking up and intensifying the golden glow of chicken fat on the surface of the borsch. After all my guilty enjoyment of cooking, and the effort of making the soup, I am not happy with it. I should have switched off the hob, the cabbage overcooked while we faffed with the luggage. The pre-cooked beetroot lacks depth of flavour and has minimal impact: I cannot taste the savoury soil it was born in. There is no dill. I know it is not up to scratch. Dad does not hide his disappointment. 'Mum should give you some tips.' I am stunned and about to retaliate, but Mum gently reprimands him and we exchange glances. The beetroot was pre-boiled, she explains, but the tomatoes I used must have been good. It's all good.

They recount their last days in Kakhovka, and their journey. They talk and talk. The route to Kherson, the region's centre, which normally takes an hour to reach by car, had taken my parents six hours. At every checkpoint, there was a slightly different type of occupier. Teeth missing, muddy and rough, swearing a lot, these were the Donetsk and Luhansk People's Republic separatists, plucked (by Russia) from the criminal world and easy to sway with bribes and the promise of power.

Then there were young Russian and Buryat boys, so young, my mother said, that some of them weren't yet shaving.

A car in front of them stopped and the young Ukrainian man at the wheel was stripped completely naked there and then. The Russians checked for 'Nazi tattoos' and any signs of combat, such as gun-bruised shoulders. Men of my father's age were spared the stripping. But a Russian FSB officer came over to my mother's window. He took her passport and studied it carefully, then he shifted his eyes into hers and held her gaze, not flinching, almost not blinking.

The most frightening thing was when she was asked her name; he had just read it in the passport. Why did he ask again? Sternly, 'What is your name?' Mum wanting to retort icily, a skill at which she is expert, along the lines of, 'You have just read my name in the passport, how dare you ask me?' But she held her tongue, remembering my instructions. 'Olga Grebenyuk' (she rolls her 'g's hard, in a Russian manner). 'What do you do?' 'I am a pensioner.' 'Do you have anything to hide?' 'No.' More prodding questions. 'Why are you leaving then?' She said simply, 'Because there is shooting.' And it was like this at every checkpoint. They passed Kherson and waited for four hours by the bridge to leave Russian-occupied territory, but they were turned back. Heavy fighting was happening ahead.

They slept that night at a friend's house and, when it was fairly safe again, set off towards Western Ukraine the next day. Later, my dad would tell us over and over again just how big a hole a missile creates and how far pieces of a blown-up tank and shrapnel fly. 'Like craters in a moon,' he said. That's what our home was becoming: a devastated moon with 50-metre-wide craters.

Suddenly Mum's face crumples; no, elongates. Her face reddens from the strain of containing emotion, but her eyes fill up and a few tears drop into the crochet tablecloth before she brusquely wipes them away. I am not sure I have ever seen my mum cry openly and fully, noisily. She has always performed this facial pantomime. However hard it hurts, she doesn't want us to see her break down. I understand this and desperately try to change the subject, to give them a break. I praise the dodgy-looking but brilliant supermercato and the Italian produce hidden within. I urge them, while they are here, to try fresh new broad beans as the Italians do, podded there and then, eaten with chunks of Pecorino on the side. I tell them that Mum must plant beetroot and dill here, otherwise the borsch will be just average, like the soup I cooked, not excellent like Mum's in Ukraine.

The light grows cooler and so does the kitchen. Dad fiddles with the wood burner. Mum gets cold easily, we joke that it's her Mediterranean blood (she has Moldovan roots). We've already eaten the borsch, the freshly made pasta and ragu, the snack bowls are empty, it is almost midnight. I keep asking Mum if they'd taken this and that from home. The sourdough starter? The tomato seeds? No, she didn't bring the seeds, she left the starter in the fridge. I think to myself, did she hope they might be back before it dies? Was it, unconsciously, a talisman? She would scoff at this idea, even if it is partly true.

She reiterates, they had to flee, they had to run for their lives, there was no leisurely making to-do and to-pack lists. In Ukraine they call it tryvozhna valiza, an 'emergency bag', and it is what every Ukrainian who decided to stay in the country packed straight after the invasion. The government even circulated a manual about what to do in case you have to flee, what to do if you are under occupation, what to do during a nuclear strike. The word tryvozhna comes from tryvoha, which means 'alarm', 'alert' or 'panic', but tryvozhna also means 'anxious', so the term tryvozhna valiza has many layers. 'The anxious bag': sounds about right.

At home, they told me, large expensive items, such as rugs and oil-painting reproductions, were hidden in someone's storage unit, Mum's car in someone else's garage. One small suitcase that they have brought with them is full of family photos, Mum and Dad's letters from the 1970s; the other of Mum's embroideries. The large bag contains their clothing. That is it. I think of a poem by Serhiy Zhadan, Ukraine's most famous contemporary poet:

> Take only what is most important. Take the letters.
> Take only what you can carry.
> Take the icons and the embroidery, take the silver,
> Take the wooden crucifix and the golden replicas.

Take some bread, the vegetables from the garden,
then leave.
We will never return again.
We will never see our city again.
Take the letters, all of them, every last piece of
bad news.

It was written in 2015. There is nothing different today.

I check if Mum knows the poem. She doesn't, and its description of a home, so similar to hers, makes her cry again. I float the idea that the words in this poem might be true for my parents' situation. What will we do then? But Dad's expression at that moment is the one I have known for as long as I can remember. The expression he had when I told him I thought our dog would die, when I doubted I would pass an exam, when I believed I wouldn't get that job. His face has the sheen of an oracle. Vse bude Ukrayina: 'It will all be Ukraine.' It will all be OK. Both of my parents believe they will be back home by the end of summer. There just cannot be any other way.

My maternal grandfather, Viktor Mardarenko, Voznesensk, 1939

2

The Great Hush

The next spring, in 2023, I am walking out of my kitchen at home in London, intent on writing. In my left fist I manage to clutch a cup of coffee, a glass of water and five fat pills that are meant to help me bring my cycle back; it vanished as soon as the war started. In my right hand, I am carrying a milk-coloured jug painted with vertical mint stripes. In it, a single sunflower.

I have just been watching footage of Kakhovka taken by a childhood friend. He was filming while he was driving, right arm hanging out of the driver's seat window: there are charred cars hollowed out by fire, craters in the road, scenes of an apocalypse. Then I watched another video, taken by a school friend's mum. A missile has hit an apartment block. It is a Khrushchevka block, built in the 1960s, where my friend's grandmother lives, and where my own grandmother Liusia lived for the last two years of her life in the early 2000s. I hate Khrushchevka apartment blocks; they are shoddily made, ugly and all look the same. But although this could be anywhere, I recognised this one and felt a heavy boulder swell up inside me, making it hard to breathe. The balcony just above Liusia's old flat is a broken Jenga of wood and plastic. The windows in most of the apartments have been blown out from the centre; jagged edges still cling to the frames, flapping like paper.

My friend Kie, who films my cooking videos, is here in the kitchen packing up his equipment. We have been filming cookery for two days. After we finish, I sit at the table quietly, watching these videos on my phone. Then I go outside to cut this dark-petalled sunflower. I pause in the door frame, to say goodbye and lament my lack of writing progress. I feel tired, I say, and every time I write about the past, I cry. I cry more when I am tired. He doesn't know that I have just been watching footage of my hometown that looks like a set for an end-of-the-world film. But he understands: his wife, my friend Nataliya, is Ukrainian. 'This,' he says in his sonorous Sunderland accent, 'you carrying this single sunflower upstairs. It's so Ukrainian. It will help you, you know. You can do it.'

I have been avoiding writing about my maternal grandmother for five months now. The rest of the book is almost finished, but this chapter is so hard to write.

I grew up with Liusia's stories. When I speak to my cousin Iryna, who is twelve years older than me, she says, 'Instead of fairytales, I lived for Liusia's stories. Even though so many of them were steeped in extreme trauma, they felt otherworldly and precious to me. Like myths or magic.' So far, I have been able to write about Liusia's garden, about joy and healing. But the suffering she endured is hard to go into. It prises open the lesions of generational trauma, intensifying that of my own. There is too much salt in the soup, too much salt in my wound.

Just a week ago, I composed a plea on Twitter, a cry for support from my online community. 'My hometown Kakhovka is being pummelled. I can't explain how much it hurts to see the destruction. Have been floored for a few days now.'

Among dozens of supportive messages, there is the troll. I normally ignore the trolls, but that night I reply. He sends me another message, plus a video of what looks like pigs eating the remnants of a Ukrainian soldier's body. I watch it and catch myself feeling numb. A year ago, seeing just a glimpse of something like this would knock me for a couple of days. But now it feels scary that I find these horror scenes 'manageable'. If that's how I feel, what are those who commit the atrocities of war feeling? How quickly do human minds get used to the horrors, how soon does dissociation and dehumanisation envelop you?

I reply to the troll again, and he retorts in a weirdly poetic and astute way. He says, 'My ancestors are smiling at me. Can you say the same?' This time I do not reply. I report and block him. I think: how interesting, even clever, of him to dig so very deep. The troll is aware of history, of our still-open wounds. I need some closure.

I start a list of occasions when I see my ancestors' smiles:

1. My children's eyes when they smile (every single day).
2. My own face in photographs, but not in the mirror (must smile at self in mirror).
3. Curves of leaves, petals, the stalk of a sunflower on my desk, fractal patterns in its seeded heart.
4. Misiats: the crescent moon.
5. Scythes held by ghosts (of my ancestors).
6. A wedge of beetroot.
7. The bird with a leaf for its wing on the front cover of the anthology of Ukrainian poets by my bedside.
8. The actual photographs of my grandparents smiling.
9. The blue-and-yellow anatomical heart knitted by a Glaswegian friend.

I decide to continue the list, and when I learn how to write poetry, to write a poem about it. I can see us smiling when we all used to get together in the summer at Liusia's house. Mum's family was big, and everybody had scattered. Her brother Viktor first went to Moscow, then Sverdlovsk, then Novosibirsk. Yura went to Moscow. Zhenia and Valia went to Dnipro to study. Slava too went to Dnipro, but after Zhenia and her husband Sasha ended up in Kakhovka, he joined them there and married a local, my aunt Liuda.

No one remained in Voznesensk near their mother Liusia. So whenever her children came to visit her, especially if they were coming from the furthest parts of the Soviet Union, those who still lived in Ukraine would try to coordinate and visit at the same time. It was the beginning of what we would end up calling, jokingly, 'The Summit', which sounds the same in Ukrainian as it does in English: Samit.

All my senses allow me to go to that place often, as it was so alive with colour, sound, texture, scent, flavour. The voices of cockerels, goats, dogs, sparrows and doves in the first part of the day and cuckoos, nightingales and crickets at dusk are loud and mix with our own. The sun scorches the village road outside the gate into pale-coloured dust, but on the other side of the gate, a watermelon sits in a bucket under a running ice-cold tap. Walk under a long living corridor of Isabella grapevines into the garden, where the trees let in just the tiniest bit of dappled light. The soil was watered in the early morning and still feels cool beneath bare feet. The blooms of the tree peonies are so heavy they should be drooping, but they don't, they stand up proud, greeting us with bright golden Cyclops eyes.

Two long tables are brought outside and covered with a crisp white cloth. Both ends are laden with drinks: 3-litre jars of homemade cherry juice – whole cherries with their stones, sunk to the bottom – home-fermented berry wines and beers for the adults. Then large round plates and oblong platters are brought out of the summer kitchen. Pyrizhky buns: kefir dough stuffed with dill and egg, or potato and caramelised onion, shallow-fried. I can hear the sound they make when they brush against each other: crispy, a delicious kind of friction. Noodles are drowned in confit goose and its juices, or ribs of pork braised with huge, winding dumplings, soaked at the bottom and steamed fluffy on top, brown-beige hues of deep, cosy flavour. But splashes of colour arrive promptly and brighten the table's canvas. Juicy sliced tomatoes glisten on oval gold-rimmed plates. Cucumbers are small and spiky. Whole bunches of herbs lie side by side, holding frilly hands: the purple of basil, the green of dill and coriander. And always pickles, even in the summer: fizzy brined tomatoes and allspice berries; pressed wrinkly aubergines stuffed with grated carrot; olive-coloured gherkins, pretty laced dill umbrellas nestled in between.

We sit and eat and drink and listen to stories, family histories. We are all extremely loud. The first time my husband heard me and Mum talking on the phone, he had to ask if we were OK, he genuinely thought we were fighting. Imagine that intensity multiplied forty times. All sorts of stories spilling out. The funny or adventure-laden tales made everyone raise their voices even louder. That's why, when the tragic stories came up, the lowering of voices was so noticeable.

When I was growing up, I never questioned why we talked about certain things in half-whispers, I just thought maybe it made the stories sound more serious, more mysterious. Only now do I understand why. For the older generation it had become a muscle memory, and us younger ones copied their whispers without thinking, a learned behaviour. My grandparents' memories were 'mined' and had to be trodden on lightly for a long time, to avoid harm. Besides, it was outright dangerous to utter what was called anti-Sovietshyna. Some of those stories were not spoken out loud until after I was born, when the full scale of Stalin's crimes was revealed in the 1980s. More and more came out, but the voices would automatically lower themselves even in 2021, the last time we were all together.

When Liusia died, we stopped getting together for a good ten years. I asked Mum why and she said this is what happens. An older generation dies, and everyone creates their own unit and splinters. I wouldn't have that, not yet. My thirtieth birthday was coming up in July 2014, and I proposed we invite everyone to my parents' house in Kakhovka and see what happened. I, once one of the babies of the family, had already been living in the UK for ten years and now had a small son of my own. A landmark birthday was a worthy excuse to make an effort.

Forty family members show up. There are so many of us that we settle in little groups throughout the garden, migrating between them. I am on a bench at the long wooden table under the pergola of the summer kitchen, in a white pinafore dress that glows against my arms and legs, spindly and dark brown this summer. Sasha sits next to me, legs dangling high above the ground. To the right is my Aunt Liuda, and Mum and my cousin Iryna sit to my left. We are at the crayfish-eating station and share the job of de-shelling the critters for Sasha as well as for ourselves. Under the tecoma blooms on the left of the terrace, my dad sits with his gammy leg, chain-smoking Vogues (I think he considers them 'healthier'). The boys – my brother, cousins, their kids – stand around him, beers in hand. To the right, the teenagers squeal, playing badminton. I can't see that far, but I know that the shuttlecock already looks like a frayed rain-soaked bird. Under the canopy of the wild grapes, where it's coolest, there is another wooden table, this one covered in an embroidered cloth. The dishes have already been whisked away and washed and dried. The older uncles, Viktor and Slava, sit at that table. Their voices are similar too, they sound like Liusia, with a slight rasp that scuffles from the lower throat when long vowels come out. After my birthday, we made a pact to get together every August and continue what had been started by Liusia: the family Samit, where we eat, drink and exchange stories, old and new.

When I started writing this book, I looked through my old laptop and phone for recordings I'd made of my family talking when I was researching summer kitchens. Summer kitchens are quite the cultural phenomenon in Ukraine: one-room outbuildings where cooking and preserving is done in the summer and early autumn. Pretty much everyone in villages and small towns has one. There are multiple voice memos made by me in Mum's garden in Kakhovka; summer kitchens turned out to be a door into other topics, other worlds and other timescapes.

The last recording was made on 23 August 2021 and I was in luck, because for this last summit a large chunk of extended family was present, including Mum's sister Valia, her brother Slava and his wife Liuda, and the eldest of Mum's five siblings, my Uncle Viktor, who we call 'the walking encyclopedia'. Viktor was freakishly erudite; whatever topic we talked about, he would give you an answer and then some, without having to look anything up online. Viktor had been writing down vignettes of our family history, and in 2018, prompted by emails from me with lots of questions about his parents and grandparents, he started writing even more. I still have those four Word documents, staring at me from a screensaver of a photograph of my spring borsch, wedged between a pea and a chive flower.

The longest of all the voice memos I recorded is one and a half hours. There is a din and a racket: loud voices and the clanking of glasses. You can almost feel the stifling August heat against our bustle. Wilfred is in my arms, a baby, and he is fussing and crying, drowning out everyone's voices. Forks stab and scrape. Then Viktor starts the story about his father, Viktor Sr. Everyone is impatient to add a detail or argue about the order of events, or the exact dates. I try to coordinate and direct, in the petulant voice of a child (I tend to regress around my family). 'Mamaaaaa, just let Vitichka tell his story.' Our voices rise higher in excited shrieks, or become eerily quiet.

By the time I started recording, we had been at the table for five hours. Mum is asking if anyone wants more food. 'How much can one eat, Mama, seriously?' 'But the children!' 'Don't get distracted, tell me about Liusia's garden in Voznesensk.' I'd heard it many times before, but I want it again, like a child asking for a favourite night-time story. 'Give me more detail this time, what would her day be like in 1968?'

Mum imitates Liusia's voice and I wonder if that makes her feel as if her mother is by her side again. Life is hard, there are many children, goats and a cow. But never does Mum fail to mention that Liusia's garden is blahorodny. Blaho means 'good' and rod is 'birth'. A 'well-bred' garden then, not necessarily manicured, but full of flowers, there to please the eye, rather than functional. Sure, there are cooking herbs and tomatoes, but all the unsightly vegetables are banished to another plot of land, an allotment by the forest. In Liusia's garden there are mostly blooms. On her way to do her daily chores, she would linger among the flowers as she passed and stop to talk to them. Mum's intonation changes. In Liusia's raspy voice, we hear, 'Moya dorohenka [my darling], are you feeling ill?' She would quietly sing to them too, her favourite songs. 'I look at the sky and think the same thought, why am I not a falcon, why hasn't God given me wings? If he did, I would leave this Earth and soar to the sky.' Mum sings softly and then, in a very good imitation of Liusia's voice, stops sharply. 'Ta sho zh tse ya rooooobliu!' 'What am I doing!? I am late to milk the cow!'

Photographs encased in neat plastic sleeves would always be brought out at our family summits. We don't have photographs of the inside of Liusia's house, but there are a few of her garden. And there they are: the roses. I think of Sleeping Beauty and her castle, hidden from the world, overgrown with ancient thorny rose trees. The photographs are black and white, but Mum remembers each of the flowers' colours and their grand-sounding names: the canary-yellow Elite, and Gloria with powder-pink edges and golden core. The best was the white rose right outside her window. In August, as Mum would wake, dozens of rambling white rose heads burst in through her open window and not even the night-time dew could dampen the warmth and strength of their perfume.

I have one of these photographs, one that Mum managed to bring with her in the suitcases when she fled Ukraine. In it, she is about two years old. She is standing underneath an unusually large window, an opening; no glass has been installed yet as Liusia and Viktor were still rebuilding. Liusia, straight-backed and smiling, stands in the window in soft focus. You can tell from her posture that she is unbelievably proud of her child and of her roses. My toddler mum squints against the glaring sun; the white rose bush – or possibly moon flower, it is hard to tell – is scrambling, sprawlingly, up the walls of the house behind her.

Photographs like these are unusual. People could not afford to own cameras at the time, but Liusia wanted a record, a record of beauty, of the garden that was already in full swing before the house was even finished, and of her sixth child, who she had late in life by the standards of the day. She was almost forty and only a few years away from becoming a grandmother. Usually, people would visit a town's photo atelier, where they would be photographed against a painted mural of a birch forest or some such, but Liusia must have wanted the real deal. She arranged for a local photographer to come to the house, to record the well-born aesthetic of her garden, her husband and her youngest child. I have that photo now in a frame on the dresser in my London bedroom, right opposite the bed. When I wake and put on my glasses, I can make out that wall, the window and the flowers – even the white-green spiders inside the flowers – and imagine the aroma of it all.

The conversations on the recording are fractured. I can hear Viktor telling my brother the story of the bear he encountered in the Altai Mountains while hiking in 1971, but I tune in to Mum, who now describes their cherry-tree blossom as a fountain. 'Fontan!' The white blossom is packed in so tightly that you couldn't make out the brown of the branches. In the summer, it bore huge yellow cherries with pink-blushed cheeks. It was a majestic tree, a real character. Mum explains the fate of the huge window, a summer kitchen annexe is built around it. But when my grandfather was building it, he came too close to the tree. He could not bring himself to cut off the thick south-facing branch that was 'in the way', so the branch was incorporated into the architecture of the annexe: it went through the wall and out the roof of the summer kitchen's veranda.

I grill Mum about all the fruit trees: 'Tell me more, there must be more.' Her voice rises in a revelatory 'Ahhhh!' There was a small peach tree that had self-seeded from a rogue stone, dropped by a child or a bird. It grew right by the wall of the veranda. Liusia spotted it and took care of the spindly little thing until it grew stronger and stronger, tall enough that its crown rested on the veranda's roof. The whole crown rested on that roof, preventing the peaches from falling to the ground. Mum and her neighbours would sling up the ladder and collect the furry fruit straight from the roof. There was a pear tree too; a taller ladder would come out and unripe fruit would be carefully picked, individually wrapped in newspaper and kept in the attic in a massive cardboard suitcase. Everyone butts in at this point of the story. We all experienced the pear suitcase, the anticipation of it being opened, the aroma of a thousand peardrop caramels hitting your nostrils, the inability to contain the juices which covered one's chin, neck, chest and even belly.

In 2018, when Joe and I went to look at what would become our London house, there was a spindly peach tree in the garden that had clearly come out of a dropped stone, as it grew right in the roots of an old established pear tree, where you would never deliberately plant a new tree. We loved the house, but seeing these two trees together almost felt like a sign: I immediately knew this would be my home. The pears were good too; not as good as Liusia's 'Duchesse d'Angoulême', but we do the same thing with them. Joe's family's old clunky suitcase is filled with newspaper-wrapped pears throughout early October. When I open the suitcase, it is 'Like I enter my childhood,' as Mum says in the voice memo.

By now there is a cacophony of voices; my cousin Aliona takes charge and firmly orders my brother and uncles to sit next to each other, rather than shout across the table. We can't hear what my mum says about the gardens. Some of them joined later and did not realise that I was recording either. Bohdan: 'Shit, have I been swearing?' 'It's not going on the bloody BBC, Bohdan, it's for research, speak freely.' 'Mum, who taught Liusia about plants then?' Mum says that Liusia had just one single book on plants. Now that we have information perpetually at the tip of our fingers, we forget how precious and hard-won it was in the past and in places such as the provincial towns of Soviet Ukraine. Then Mum pauses, breathes in, and a long high-pitched, rolling sigh comes out and ends as an 'Oyyyyy', the sound one makes in pain, like ouch, but also in disdain or disappointment or resignation. As a teenager, Liusia had found a job in a flower nursery, and we think working in the garden helped her heal. Because there is a dark side to this story.

Liusia's maiden name was Bezchastna. Letter combinations hint at bez, 'without', and shchastya, 'happiness'. Liusia Sans-joy, of sorts. She was born in 1921, at the height of the civil war and the end of the first big famine. Given how close we were to Liusia, it is frustrating that we know so little about the early years of her father, Moisei Ivanovich Bezchastnyi. It is very possible that we don't know much because he never talked about it. Liusia mentioned two things: that he returned to Ukraine from Siberia and that he served in the Russian Imperial Navy during the First World War. She always used the phrase povernulys z Sybyriu, 'they returned from Siberia'.

Why was he in Siberia, and how did he come back to Ukraine? Was Moisei born in exile? Was he born in Besarabia, near the Black Sea, is that why he went into the navy? Was he part Polish? The ending of his surname hints at that. Or Jewish, as his name Moisei — Moses — suggests? He named one of his sons Yakov, a more commonly Jewish than traditionally Ukrainian name. Liusia herself used Yiddish phrases often, especially with us children when we were being particularly anarchical. 'Meshuggener kop!', she used to shout, 'silly head'. 'This is the very tsimmes!' she would say, meaning 'this is the real deal', though there was never any actual tsimmes (an Ashkenazi dish from Southern

Ukraine with root vegetables and dried fruit) cooked at home. If there were connections to Ashkenazi culture, they must have been buried deep for safety, after the Tsarist and Bolshevik pogroms.

One fact is clear: Moisei returned to Ukraine after the First World War with a maimed leg. In the future, he will not like my grandfather, Viktor. He will suspect him of being too good-looking not to be a philanderer. The dislike will be mutual and Viktor would often have a dig, half-jokingly, 'That maimed leg, Lyusenka, was samostrel!' (a self-inflicted wound). Whatever the truth, like our collective trauma, the wound in Moisei's leg kept reopening. His first wife died soon after he returned, and he was left alone with their three children, the eldest, Vira, and two boys Hrygory (Hrysha) and Yakov (Yasha). It was tough to look after three children with a wound that wouldn't heal.

At this point they lived in Besarabia, a region since integrated into Odesa, by the Romanian border, and he married my great-grandmother, a Moldovan-Ukrainian widow called Yaryna Kolchak. Yaryna had two children of her own, Marusia and Volodymyr. Yaryna was petite, like an egret, and in contrast to Moisei's deep-olive skin that turned maroon in the summer, hers was porcelain-white. This is all I know about what she looked like. I wish I knew more, as out of all my great-grandparents she feels the closest to me in spirit, because of her famous cooking style. The legend goes that she simply could not bring herself to economise, not meaning that she was wasteful, but that she liked to cook deliciously. Her motto was, 'Eat well today, fast tomorrow'. She found it hard to water things down, or to make things stretch. She would rather make a delicious meal and then skip a day of eating than skimp on the amount of fat and salt that was essential to make the food taste good.

Moisei, who was extremely economical and money-conscious, used to lament, 'Yaryyyyna, you will bankrupt me, Yarynaaaaa.' There is a very specific way that my family mimics this sentence while telling the story. I can hear it now, a guttural and elongated, dramatically desperate 'Yaryyyyna'. An intonation that Liusia mimicked, then her children mimicked and has now been recorded by me. It has survived for a hundred years already, just through our voices. And now it's splattered on my screen, like a squashed caterpillar.

Soon after they married, Moisei and Yaryna had a daughter called Lida, and soon after that, when the cherries were ripening in June, Liusia was born. She was born on the day of Holy Trinity, a fact of which she never failed to remind us. Holy Trinity is a holiday, like Easter, that doesn't have a fixed date, so it was special to be born on this important religious occasion and Liusia felt her birthday was a lucky day, a good sign. After all, her family survived the calamity that came soon after.

The history of Ukraine between 1917 and 1924 is mind-bogglingly complicated. Before the Russian Revolution, Ukraine was split between the Russian and different empires for hundreds of years. After the

Revolution, it was fought over by the Red Army, the tsarist White Army, the anarchical Black Army, imperial Germany and groups led by both Ukrainian students and intellectuals as well as by West Ukrainian militants. Between 1917 and 1920, four separate Ukrainian republics were formed and dissolved. They say that, in 1919, in one of Kyiv's county administration buildings, they held at least three official portraits at the ready – of Taras Shevchenko (the father of Ukrainian identity), Alexander III (the Russian emperor) and Lenin (the Bolshevik leader) – to use tactically, to display whichever would be most relevant and life-saving in any particular sticky situation. It was chaos. Eventually, Ukraine was annexed on 30th December 1922, and became part of the Soviet Union.

In the summer after Liusia was born, a cataclysmic drought hit the grain-producing areas of what was soon to become the USSR. Southern Ukraine and South Russian Povolzhye were affected worst of all. The provisional government in Moscow ordered the confiscation of 26 million kilos of Ukrainian grain and exported it; the grain represented all the reserves that would have saved millions of Ukrainian lives. Close to 3.5 million people died in Southern Ukraine between Liusia's birth and the day that she spoke her first proper sentence. Those who survived either had links to the Communist Party, or hid their resources well, as Moisei must have done. People hid grain and potatoes in reeds, using local spots that Communist commissars would not know about.

Two Soviet policies and their abrupt reversal were particularly important to Liusia's story. One was called NEP – Lenin's New Economic Policy – and the other, Korenizatsia: Indigenisation or Ukranianisation.

The NEP had elements of state-controlled free market capitalism. It was a bid to give the struggling Soviet economy the kiss of life. It was not so easy to transform the backwards Russian Empire into a proletariat paradise in just four years, bearing in mind that the whole world had just come out of a catastrophic war. The NEP gave one the freedom to work for oneself. We think that Moisei must have grabbed the opportunity and bought some land on which to grow crops. So when Liusia turned two, the family moved to Rakove village, near Voznesensk, on the left side of the South Buh River.

Rakove is an area as soft and round as a golden dome of sweet, yeasted bread. The landscape around the South Buh River is both gentle and dramatic. The gentleness comes from the curve of the river itself, the dip of the valley, golden-haired, emerald-stemmed reeds and the voluptuous shrubs mimicking the shapes of the clouds above them. Weeping willows drink from the river, creating blueish-green rooms under the canopy of their arched, floppy branches. Small clay houses painted Moldovan blue punctuate the smooth squiggle of the dirt road. The name Rakove comes from rak, which means 'crayfish', and indeed the South Buh River is teeming with the critters, caught by local boys, which to this day are sold in buckets on the side of the road.

I have passed through Rakove many times, and even though I do not know for sure what their house looked like, I try to imagine it. In my mind, Moisei and Yaryna's house is painted a deep blue. There is a well, also painted blue and with a green iron spool. I know that the house, like most others in the village, stood right on top of a slope which stretched down for a good 200 metres, all the way to the river, flanked by strips of reeds. This south-facing slope was covered in small, pig-tailed watermelons, and it was called bashtan. They say bashtan comes from the Turkic word bostan for 'melon garden', and in Ukrainian, the word evolved to mean a plot of land used specifically for growing all sorts of melons.

The sun was always in the zenith where Moisei's bashtan was located. It simply could not be a more perfect location for watermelons, which need all the sun they can get, and his harvest was always plentiful. But their main livelihood came from wheat fields, which demanded a lot of attention and real toil. Both parents and all the children, apart from the baby of the family, Liusia, worked hard, from dawn to late evening. Most of the year they managed without help, but when it came to sowing and harvest, Moisei employed local people, he paid for their labour and fed them. Viktor's notes say that the family had three horses, a plough and a mower. Within ten years, Moisei was a relatively prosperous farmer.

The NEP was closely linked to another Soviet policy: Korenizatsia. Korenizatsia is often translated as 'indigenisation', which isn't incorrect. However, it is important to note that korenizatsia has the word korinnya in it: 'root'. So in Ukrainian, 'indigenous people' is korinne nasellennya, or literally, 'root people'. Korenizatsia was about 'rooting in', a policy of self-identification, and it was allowed to take place in various spheres of Ukraine's cultural life. It was billed as freedom, a benevolent, wise policy, a show of respect and understanding from magnanimous brother Russia towards its 'little siblings' Ukraine, the Baltic States, Belarus and Central Asia. It was an attempt to show the resistant indigenous population that the Soviet Ukrainian Republic was not ruled by occupiers, but by the people. The Russian Empire had been the enslaver, but the Soviet Union was the liberator. Unchain yourselves! Speak your own language!

Korenizatsia sparked a cultural renaissance, especially in the new capital of Ukrainian USSR, Kharkiv, which quickly changed from a provincial town to a cultural and avant-garde centre. It gave rise to an artistic modernism that drew on Ukrainian folk culture and the traditional practices of embroidery, folk painting, storytelling and song to create a fresh new vision of the world.

Lenin, who understood the 'national question' very well, had decided that, to begin with at least, it was better to allow freedom when it came to self-identification, as it could reduce friction and possible uprisings. Too fast an erasure of one's culture, language and sense of self was too dangerous. So, for at least a decade, they were not disturbed. Liusia and her siblings were able to root in. They could speak the Ukrainian language, sow wheat and plant their bare feet in the black earth of Rakove. But in 1924, following a series of strokes, the architect of the Soviet state and the policy of indigenisation died and his biggest fear — Stalin's accession — became reality.

Lenin and Stalin had fought viciously over the 'automisation' of the numerous Soviet republics. Lenin had favoured a relaxed union of the republics, united militarily and in foreign policy terms. But Stalin wanted the Soviet Union to be controlled from Moscow. Despite being ethnically Georgian, Stalin was a great Russian chauvinist, who famously called Russians the greatest people 'before all'. In 1929, he reversed Lenin's NEP and Korenitzatsia in favour of state centralisation, Russification and a commitment to rigid, ideology-flavoured social realism in culture. No more modernisation, no more innovations, no more thought or expression that trickled behind the rigid line of Soviet Communist doctrine.

In 1930, the 16th Congress of the Russian Communist Party ruled that industrialisation and collectivisation were to be rolled out. Smallholdings were required to be absorbed into collective farms. The process pretended to be a kind of choice: those who agreed to give up their land and grain could join a collective farm. But those who refused were murdered, or forcibly dispossessed and sent to labour camps, or deported. Those who joined collective farms survived for a while, but the system was brutal even towards them. Until the 1960s, if you worked on a collective farm, you worked for what was called trudoden, from trud, 'labour', and den, 'day'. An expression emerged, to work for palychky, which means both 'tick' and 'stick': a tick for each day you worked, like clocking in and out. Each of these 'sticks' was supposed to be exchanged for 120 grams of grain. A lot of the time, people worked for a whole year, amassing many 'sticks', but were not paid at all. We assume that Moisei refused to give up his land and animals in order to work at the collective farm for sticks.

A propaganda poster from that time depicts a stunted farmer holding the reins of an exhausted, starved horse dragging a plough, looking up at rosy-cheeked collective farm workers and at a man wearing a budyonovka, the pointed, red-starred Bolshevik army hat. The farmer peers through a bold red question in Ukrainian: 'Why have you not joined the kolhozp [collective farm] yet?'

The Soviets had to bring out the big guns. Holodomor. It comes from two words: holod, 'famine', and moryty, 'to exterminate by exhaustion'. Holodomor was Stalin's war on Ukrainian peasants. More Ukrainian people died during this war than during the First World War. The victims were mostly women, children and older people. People in the countryside were prohibited from having passports (which you needed to move freely around the country) and so they were effectively banned from leaving their villages. While people were besieged, and died in the streets from starvation, confiscated Ukrainian wheat was sold abroad at dumping prices.

In an autobiographical story called *His Secret*, the Ukrainian writer Arkadiy Lyubchenko describes what he found when he went into the countryside to investigate the rumours that had reached him in Kharkiv. There was a blood-chilling silence. Not only could you not hear the usual sounds of farm animals, there were no barking dogs, no meowing cats. The village was muzzled by hunger. Women, children and the elderly were dying in the streets. 'The last drop of kerosene has been used a while ago, it has been a long time since they'd eaten all cats and dogs. It was not a village looming before us, but a silent cemetery where some of the living dead still lingered.'

Peasants were divided into three categories: bednyaks (poor), serednyaks (making ends meet) and kurkuls (more prosperous farmers). My family fell into the last category for the simple reason that they occasionally hired a helping hand. If they had money to pay others to work for them, they had an excess, so they were 'enemies of the people'. Moisei's house and farmland in Rakove were confiscated, his stored grain, his animals and his house, and he was put into a local prison. Yaryna and the seven children, including nine-year-old Liusia, were to be 'repatriated'.

'Repatriation' was the word used by the Soviets to describe forced resettlement. Later on, the term changed to the word for deportation. But I feel like the words 'deportation', even 'forced deportation' or 'exile', do not explain adequately what happened to Liusia and thousands of others. They are officious and abstract terms and don't represent the experience in its horrific fullness. The word to describe what happened to Liusia would have to be very loaded, as it would have to encompass the following: being made homeless (dispossession), being forcibly removed from your hometown or village (abduction/kidnapping), being transported in inhumane conditions thousands of kilometres away from your home and family (human trafficking).

I asked on Twitter what word would be best to use, which was loaded enough to convey the meaning. 'Cleared?' It was good but not quite there. 'Transhumed?' That gave me the chills. People from all over the world replied. The word in Latvian is izsūtījums, in Finnish it's küüditamine, in Lithuanian tremtis, in Crimean Tatar sürgün. French Canadians mentioned the forced deportation of Acadians and used the phrase Le Grand Dérangement, 'The Great Upheaval'. They all mean either 'deportation' or 'exile', but the words themselves are loaded with history. The people who speak those various languages immediately understand what is meant: dispossession, abduction, human trafficking, then either imprisonment and forced labour – essentially slavery – or abandonment to die or survive in a climatically hostile foreign environment, so far away from home you cannot be rescued by those who have been left behind. 'Deportation' in English is too formal a word, which hints at something to do with law.

There was no law here. Just people who were robbed, murdered, deported or starved. The term they used in Russian was even worse, na poselenie, literally 'to make a settlement'. There was no settle in this settlement, more of an uprooting, a complete de-indigenisation.

Liusia and her mother and siblings were packed with many others into a cattle train and sent to the northern part of the Vologda region in Russia, close to the southern Finnish province of Karelia. Understandably, Liusia didn't talk about it much and I try my best not to imagine it too often. But here is an account of the journey from my friend Katrya Kalyuzhna from Kakhovka, whose grandparents Kateryna Polshchan and Ivan Kyrychenko were 'dekurkulised' by the Bolsheviks from the Kherson oblast in a similar scenario. 'They were sent in trains to Arkhangelsk region, also in winter. A lot of children died on the way. But true hell unravelled when they got to their destination. Dead, frozen children, from nought to twelve, were piled on top of each other, like logs. My grandfather Ivan had to sort through these children, desperately looking for his little sister who had ended up in a different carriage and was lost. She wasn't in the pile of log children. It turned out that she froze during the journey, her body thrown off the moving train before it reached its destination.' I try not to think of these frozen driftwood children, but they do haunt me, like they haunted Kateryna, Ivan, Yaryna, Liusia and thousands of others.

My grandmother was lucky. She did not freeze and I will never know what Yaryna had to do to prevent that from happening. They made it alive to the final destination, which was in the middle of nowhere in the dead of winter. They were thrown off the train, but not at a station, nor even a stop, but straight into the snow of the dark, bloated belly of a Russian forest. If she kept the horrors of the journey hidden from us, this was the part where Liusia allowed herself to put some flesh on the bones of her story. She would widen her eyes and move her head, as if she was watching the blizzard rage around them. I always imagined this part cartoonishly, like a woodblock illustration in a children's book, blue whorls of a tempest, like frozen waves of an ocean. She told us how immediately all the women and children knelt in the snow, foreheads against the freezing ground, urgent prayers stage-whispered between their lips and the earth. Their breath melting the snow, the wail of the wind now loud, now smothered by the padded room of frosted pines. The older boys and the old men went in search of help. Liusia was not religious (it was safer not to be since the Bolsheviks had arrived), but when she told the story it was clear she believed that their prayers led the men straight to an Old Believer monastery. They were not in complete isolation, there were people who could give them shelter and food. I wonder if the existence of a branch of the Orthodox Church whose members have been persecuted in Russia since the seventeenth century, and were being actively persecuted by the Communists during the 1930s purges, shows just how remote was the place they were deposited into.

Yaryna and the children survived initially by digging in a zemlyanka. Zemlyanka comes from the word zemlya: 'earth'. It was literally an earth house, a dug-out, the main body of which was buried with only one-third of the house sticking out of the ground with a tiny door. Twelve-year-old Liusia went to beg by the church in the village. One day, a woman approached her and said, 'Child, if you are going to beg, do so correctly. I will teach you. You are by a church, so don't just say, "Kind people, please give me something to eat." Say, "Kind people, please give me something to eat, in the name of Christ."' She then dipped her finger in some saliva and painted tears under Liusia's lower eyelids. The mention of Jesus and her sticky wet eyes did the trick and people started giving Liusia bits of food and some kopecks.

After her stint at begging, Liusia found a job as a nanny to a local Communist Party leader's toddler. How? We don't know. She did say that they were kind to her. And she (always) rushed to add that, in spite of being more comfortable in this family's home, which was heated and where she was fed, she still ran away at night, wading through the dreaded black snow to be with her mother, who had found work at a flax-processing plant and was now living in a communal workhouse near the factory. The older brothers, teenagers when they arrived, worked logging the forests. Uncle Viktor's notes state, 'They spent five years in Vologda region, uprooting forests and teaching the locals how to grow rye. One of Liusia's brothers, Hrysha, disappeared while in exile. He was most probably killed for disobedience at the lumberyard. Or perhaps he ran away and perished. The youngest, Yasha, married a local woman and only returned to Voznesensk in the 1960s.'

Moisei had no idea what had happened to his family or where they had been 'resettled' to. He certainly had no idea that they had been taken 2,000 kilometres away. He was going through his own hell on Earth. Imprisoned for being a kurkul, he was preparing himself for a possible trip to a far-away gulag when the wound in his leg, uncared for, developed gangrene. He could not work and he became a useless prisoner. They did not want to feed an invalid, not that there was much to feed anyone. Holodomor was in full swing when they released him on to the streets of Voznesensk, with a festering wound.

Like so many others, Moisei lay on the street lifeless and bloated. Astonishingly, however, he was spotted by a doctor. Dr Bachursky was a well-regarded surgeon in Voznesensk and had treated Moisei's leg wound in the 1920s. Whenever Liusia or Mum told this part of the story, their voices changed. They became quieter, soft as velvet, full of respect for the man, his profession, and for what he did for my great-grandfather. Dr Bachursky, who had been given food by the authorities – presumably because he was the only doctor left in the area – picked Moisei up from the street and took him to the hospital. He hid him in the quarantine section, where patients were dying from typhoid fever which was raging once again, just as it had during the famine in the 1920s.

The special volunteer 'brigades', sent to the villages by the Communist Party to take every last piece of grain from the villagers, avoided the hospital quarantine rooms. The stench of typhoid, bile and blood seeping through starving people's intestines acted as a great deterrent. Bachursky amputated Moisei's leg, gave him clean water and scraps of food. Miraculously, Moisei survived.

Some time in 1937, Yaryna returned to Rakove with five of the children. I searched far and wide to find out whether there was a decree that allowed them to return home, but I found nothing. There was no official pardon from Stalin; in fact people were still being repressed. Then it dawned on me. There was no need for Yaryna and her children to be officially 'de-resettled', because they had not been officially 'resettled' in the first place. There had been no process, no court, no documentation. They were simply loaded on to a train and, days later, thrown off the track by the edge of a forest in the dark. The lack of officialdom may have helped them to return. Besides, Stalin may have exceeded his quota of death. So many people were murdered by starvation during Holodomor that there was a shortage of workers. Officials may have closed their eyes to any 'unauthorised' returns, to replenish the numbers.

We don't quite know what happened next. We think that when the Germans occupied Southern Ukraine in 1941, Moisei became a starosta, a 'village elder'; a collaborator, in other words. Romanians controlled the left side of the Buh River, where Rakove lay, and the Germans were in Voznesensk, on the right-hand side of the river. Perhaps because Yaryna was half-Moldovan, and she spoke Romanian, Moisei was a natural choice for the Romanians. Viktor's notes say: 'Moisei was widely respected in the village back from the NEP years, and was picked by the community as the village leader. He was able to save many from the Nazis. He would have been considered a Nazi collaborator by the Soviets, so he ended up fleeing to Romania after the war. He and possibly Yaryna would have been executed by the Soviets. He lived with Yaryna in Romania, and even set up a small fabric shop which sold textiles and leather, until his death in 1958 or 1959. Before he died, he instructed Yaryna to sell their shop and use the money to bribe herself back into Ukraine. Other than that, we don't know much about his last years, as Yaryna kept shtum for the fear of being exposed and repressed again. Though she did not have to keep her secrets for long, as she died within a year of returning to Ukraine.'

I try to imagine the Beschastnys' reunion on their return. None of them knew whether the others were alive or dead. And then they meet. I started writing this paragraph imagining 'the joy of reunion'... and then I thought about it and really tried to imagine. And in my mind's eye it suddenly looks subdued. I just cannot imagine them being loud and ecstatic. I can see only silence, tears perhaps, maybe a really tight and long hug, but mostly silence.

The anti-Sovietshyna purges continued at the end of the 1930s. Most of the Ukrainianisers, including Ukrainian language teachers, were accused of fabricated crimes and repressed. The writers and artists of the Ukrainian renaissance sparked by Korenizatsia were murdered en masse. Those who did not agree to create works amenable to the Soviet doctrine were picked off one by one. Some were taken to Solovki Special Purpose Camp on the Solovetsky Islands in the White Sea, perversely created on the site of a Russian Orthodox monastery complex, where they were kept in appalling conditions. Some were sent to work on the White Sea–Baltic Canal. Between August 1937 and December 1938, people from all over the USSR were shipped to the Karelian island of Sandarmokh. There they were made to dig trenches, then lined up in front of them and shot in the back of the head. In the late 1990s, 6,241 bodies were found at the site. This was one of the many massacres perpetrated by Stalin's regime. It is estimated that more than a million people were murdered in that year alone.

It was the beginning of the Great Hush, what my grandparents called molchanka, from the Russian verb molchat, 'to be silent'. Were stories told in whispers later, as Moisei and the family settled back in? Were they whispered under the covers at night? There was huge stigma attached to having been imprisoned, or dispossessed: the stamp 'enemy of the people' could damage your life and your children's future. So there could not be any jubilation at their reunion, or a feast to mark the occasion, while Ukraine's past and present remained steeped in death like a silent cemetery.

My maternal grandmother Liusia Mardarenko, and children from left to right – Zhenia, Valia, Slava and Viktor

3

Three Thousand Eggs

One of my last memories of Liusia is of giving her a bath. We are in the bathroom in her flat in Kakhovka, the one that was in the Khrushchevka apartment block which now has a missile hole in it.

In the dim glow of the ancient light bulb, the bathroom is orange-lit. It smells of hard soap and damp. The water is so hot that steam rises up in small clouds, dulling the bright fuchsia of Mum's nails as they help to undo the buttons of Liusia's house dress. Next, her hands hold Liusia firmly but gently around one shoulder and under one armpit. Liusia's skin is loose around her arms, but you can tell there had once been a twist of strong muscle that heaved buckets, little children and huge pots of soup. Liusia's lower body is in the hot foaming water and her upper body sits up straight, so straight.

Mum says, 'Why don't you scrub Busia's back?' I move towards the rear of the bath, look more closely at Liusia's back and gasp. How strong and smooth it is; not an eighty-year-old's back, this is a young back. I touch her skin: it's so taut. I exclaim, 'Babushka, how smooth your skin is! It is so beautiful!' I lather up the bar of soap and rub the foam over her shoulders and shoulder blades, gently massaging them with my knuckles as I go. Maybe it is now exaggerated in my memory, but I see her back as colossal, broad and strong, even vertiginous. The polished back of a goddess of battle and dawn.

Years later, on a visit to Georgia, Liusia's back begins to make more sense. In Georgia they have a word, dedakatsi, which literally means 'mother-man'. It is a word used to describe (usually older) women, especially the generation of women who held things together after the Second World War. While the men were away fighting, women became the breadwinners as well as the caretakers and carers. When the men came back, just like my grandfather Viktor, ravaged by physical and mental trauma, the women continued in those roles. The Georgian women had that same posture as Liusia, the same kind of broad, solid back. Posture matters: we carry our burdens on our shoulders and backs.

This is how I remember the visits to Liusia's flat with Mum. We walk up a flight of stairs ascending from a dark but freshly painted communal entrance, then ring the loose, yellowing bell button. It sounds insect-like: dzzzzz. A pause, some shuffling, then the ghost of a booming raspy voice, 'Olechka, ty?' 'Is it you, Olia?' We go in and take off our shoes to be handed slippers, which I always try to refuse, to no avail. No slippers means I might catch a cold and die, even in the summer. So these big clunky sliders go on and a whole lot of vowels follow, the excited 'oohs' and 'ahhhs' and the dorohenky, 'my dears', and the rybochky, 'little fish'.

We ask how she is and she retorts with her invariable 'Tsvitu i pakhnu' ('I bloom and smell like a flower'), followed by a laugh. Her eyelids are permanently heavy now, eyes tired and murky, but her cheerful words about flowers lend them a glint. Even though she had to leave her smallholding with all the flowers, back in the village, she carried a garden within her. Within a day of moving into the new flat, there were potted geraniums and calendula on the balcony and she always bought cut flowers from vendors at the market. And despite the laboured shuffle and the hooded eyes, she did bloom; always neat, her thin, frost-white hair clipped by a similarly white hairpiece – to make her hair seem fuller – into a bun. The triple-mirrored dressing table had travelled from her old house with her. On it, a tube of cream, bearing the outline of two delicate hands, like a 1930s fashion croquis. When Mum and I began doing aerobics, just as the first classes in our region started in the 1990s, we would tell her about our 'shaping' lessons. She used to ask, with a quick, urgent energy, 'Olechka, am I doing it right?' and would swiftly lift her leg up and touch it with the opposite hand, then repeat with the other.

I realise now just how important those visits to her flat were. It would be just the three of us. As much as I loved the whole banda ('gang') getting together, everyone wanted to speak all at once, so stories were constantly interrupted or contested, or it was just difficult to follow when so many conversations were happening at once. During these quieter visits, we would make some tea with slices of lemon, and, more often than not, get Liusia into her fold-out bed in the living room-cum-bedroom. She would lie on the large square pillow and Mum would cover her with a thin wool blanket. We would have a quick catch-up on school and boyfriends – she loved to hear about both in equal measure – and we would dive into her memories. Mum and I now agree we should have written notes, clarified events and asked so many more questions, forensic questions. The spaces between my ribs tighten: what an oversight! But who knew then that there would be writing, or war?

In 1937, Liusia is sixteen, but she no longer lives with her parents, who remain in Rakove. Rakove is on the left bank of the Buh River and Liusia lives 6.3 kilometres away, in Voznesensk, on the right bank of the river. Farming was no longer an option, as their land no longer belonged to them. All the children had to work, to support themselves and their parents. She found a job at a flower nursery, and, later, at a vegetable canning factory, where she worked during the German occupation. I try to imagine, what was she like at the flower nursery? Is that where she learned how to talk and sing to flowers?

A food-grower friend uses three words to describe the process of propagating a rose. She says it is something you embark on with 'faith, hope and luck'. She says that you do not know whether the roots will take; it all happens under cover of darkness, within the soil. I can imagine sixteen-year-old Liusia cutting the soft wood and pushing one of its ends into gritty soil, keeping it watered and covered. She hopes and hopes and hopes that the leaves won't die, and that when she gently tugs on the plant a month later, it will tug back, telling her there are roots developing underneath. A rough-looking stick, within just a month, with enough faith, hope and luck, will have roots anchoring it to the soil; then, soon enough, tender arms with soft thorns dancing as they grow, then small buds swelling, unfurling, blooming and scenting the air.

By the time she is nineteen, Liusia has met Viktor, my grandfather. When I think of Viktor, I think of two men: the Ukrainian dissident poet Vasyl Stus and the American actor James Dean. To me, Viktor looked like a cross between the two: the fair colouring of Dean and the sharp architectural angles of Stus's face. Thick, honey-hued hair and icy blue eyes, a dimpled chin, wide cheekbones and a broad, strong nose, like a Greek statue.

Liusia was beautiful, with a nose with delicate nostrils and grey eyes framed by two raven-dark eyebrows. Her hair was almost black, woven into tight waves as if she plaited it every night before going to bed. She was on the sturdier side, with a round face that revealed little of her exquisite bone structure and a body full of breasts, belly and hips, but with that distinct waist-to-hip ratio that was pleasing, whatever her weight. It was to do with all the full-fat sour cream she used to eat by the spoonful, Mum says. Only once had she looked thinner, in a photograph from 1947. She always said she was thin in that photo because she was ill at the time. Now that I know so much more, I can calculate the dates and realise these must have been the post-war hunger years. But she does not look gaunt. Her cheekbones are high and wide, her chin is dimpled deeply, almost splitting it in two. Her eyes look light, almost ghostly in contrast to the black brows, lashes and dark circles, and she's squinting, giving her face an expression of tired defiance. The dark circles — whether they are of her illness or her hunger, I don't know — make it look like she is wearing smoky make-up. Liusia was tall, and when she wore heels, she and Viktor were the same height. They were quite the couple. The women in our family always said it was unusual that Viktor, who was nine years older than Liusia, was still single at the age of twenty-eight. He was an ancient bachelor, by the standards of the time.

Liusia said that she was attracted to her opposite, so she had noticed his blond locks a mile off. But Viktor and his brother Shura were also among the few men in town who could drive and made good money. They wore leather jackets: everyone noticed them. Viktor often joked that Liusia was the one who 'chased' him, and she would laugh and rebuke him loudly, 'Who chased who!' to which Viktor – with a smile and crinkle in the corner of his eyes – would retaliate softly, 'OK, maybe you didn't chase me, but you definitely followed me.' They met at a dance in Voznesensk. There were no nightclubs, cabarets or speakeasies in provincial Ukraine. I imagine the dance happening outside, in the Ostrovsky Park, by the nineteenth-century royal rotunda where a band would play. But most likely it went on in a local Dom Kultury, a cultural club. A Soviet culture club plaque from the 1930s reads:

Rules of conduct during dancing

- Comrades should attend dance evenings in light clothing and footwear. It is forbidden to dance in work clothes and sportswear.
- It is forbidden to dance in a distorted way.
- The dancer must perform the dance correctly, precisely following the steps with the left and the right foot.
- The woman has a right to politely express her dissatisfaction regarding the man's designation distance of 3 centimetres and to politely demand an explanation if he veers too close.
- It is forbidden to laugh and to smoke in non-designated areas.

What a convoluted way to say 'No canoodling'. I wonder how much of this was actually implemented or adhered to. I cannot imagine any 3-centimetre distance between Liusia and Viktor and I hope they laughed and smoked on the dance floor while waltzing wildly, hands and legs flailing as if they were made out of rubber! They married quickly. From Liusia's point of view, there was no time to waste – 'when you know, you know' – and if Viktor had waited until twenty-eight and hadn't wanted to marry anyone until he met her, it must be fate.

There are so many gaps in the stories of Liusia and Viktor. Sometimes I feel as though I have little scraps of a monumental jigsaw. I picture in my mind's eye the artist Alla Horska's *Tree of Life* mosaic from 1967: I have all the pieces representing the bird on top of the tree, but only a few scarlet jigsaw pieces from the base of the tree trunk.

What did I know about Viktor's family? Viktor mentioned that his father, Stepan Mardarenko, had Magyar Hungarian roots, and that his mother, Yelizaveta (Liza) Sarazhyn, came from a family of stovpovi dvoriany, a term for noble families of ancient standing. Stovp literally means 'column' and refers to a list of feudal surnames that were recorded from as early as the seventeenth century. He told us she came from a small village near Voznesensk called Dvoryanka, which means 'noble woman'. When I started researching our family history in 2018, I searched the internet over and over again for 'Sarazhyn, Dvoryanka village, Mykolayiv oblast'. I thought, because the surname was unusual and the village so specific, I would find at least a scrap of information. But to no avail. Ukrainian heritage websites hadn't yet taken off, while Western heritage websites showed results from European or American sources, but none from Soviet or Russian Empire archives. But I always trusted Viktor's story; there was no point in him making anything up, especially when the information might have been harmful to the family during the Soviet era. Then, in 2023, I decided to google the name and village again, just in case something had changed; since the war started, there had been a deluge of Ukrainians trying to find and preserve information about their roots. I stumbled across a man called Rostislav Mardarenko who was looking for information on Yelyzaveta Mykhaylivna Sarazhyn, born in 1888 in Mykolayiv oblast. Apart from using the soft letter 's' rather than 'z' in Liza's first name, everything matched. I found Rostislav's email and reached out. Within a couple of hours he replied.

He wrote in Ukrainian. 'Good evening, Oliu! I found scans of Yelyzaveta's birth certificate in regional archives through the Family Tree website. Here it is attached.' I opened the attachment called 'Metric Books, Nikolayev, 1770–1930', and in Russian cursive, so ornate it is almost illegible, was the information. Born 2 August 1888. Baptised 8 September 1888. Mostovoye town, Domanevsky region. Parents: Dvoryanin Mykhailo Ioannov Sarazhyn and his lawful wife Domnikiia

Yakovleva, both Orthodox. Godparents: Bendersky odnodvorets Andrey Dmitriev Izbash and wife of another Bendersky odnodvorets Petr Izbash, Olga Onisimova.

I quickly telephone Mum. Heirloom embroideries and an odd photograph would have been all people might have been able to hold on to from the past, and often not even that. So much personal history was lost when one's house was lost. Documents would most certainly be lost, destroyed or moved to Moscow after the break-up of the Soviet Union. So we had largely resigned ourselves to never having a physical, written confirmation of most of our personal history. Late that evening, Mum sent me a voice note. 'I cannot sleep,' she says. 'Today I found out the names and surnames of my great-grandparents. Thank you for doing this.'

Rostislav, a historian by education and a seasoned heritage hunter, gives me more tips on searching for information. He also explains that women's maiden names were not included, so Yakovleva means daughter of Yakov, not Liza's mother's surname. Within an hour, however, I find my grandfather Viktor's birth certificate, and it describes his father, my great-great-grandfather, the joie de vivre gambler Stepan Andreyevich Mardarenko, as a Bendersky meshchanin, a tradesman from a Moldovan fortress city called Bender. Suddenly, some of the snippets of information shared by Viktor and Liusia make more sense.

Liusia said that, unlike her mother Yaryna, Liza was parsimonious and a lousy cook. To sauté potatoes in a pan tastily, plenty of oil has to be used, to make them plump with crispy edges. But Liza used a tiny amount of oil and lots of water. She didn't season her food properly either. We always wondered if being so anxiously economical was a result of having lost her wealth. But now I wonder if Liza's family perhaps had a cook, and that she never in fact learned how to cook herself.

Viktor said that his father, Liza's husband Stepan Mardarenko, was a dandy and a gambler before the First World War. They owned some land and hired people from Poltava, in Central Ukraine, to work it. At the end of the harvest, when the work was done, Stepan would go on a week-long binge. He loved restaurants and high-society life, squandered money and played bridge in salons. When he was spent and out of funds, he would turn up back at their house at dawn, riding a chetyriohkolka (four-wheel-drive cart), shouting, 'Lizaaaaa, open the gate! Your husband is home!' He was draped in silk offcuts, for Liza to make herself a new dress and forgive him. Like Moisei, he went to fight in the First World War and survived, but not unscathed. During, or soon after, his return, he caught tuberculosis. The summer of 1918 was hot and six-year-old Viktor was made to stand by his father's bed and swat the flies around Stepan's yellowing features. It was scorching and the job laborious and boring. Stepan kept spitting blood, then wheezed, 'Don't worry, son. You won't have to endure this much longer. Your daddy will be dead soon.'

Yelyzaveta had four children with Stepan. Three boys, Oleksandr, Volodymyr and Viktor, and a girl called Olga. Viktor said the little girl was adored, and bonnie, but she only lived a year. Her death was a great tragedy for the family. She was the original Olia, and Viktor named his youngest daughter, my mum, after his dead sister. Liza, who was grieving for both her husband and child, decided the best survival strategy following Stepan's death was to marry his younger, unmarried brother. It was a common thing to do, keeping it in the family. They had another boy together, called Yevhen.

I have two portraits of Yelyzaveta, but have only recently found out how we inherited them. Mum says that, when her eldest uncle Oleksandr died, she was a student and missed his funeral. She went to visit his widow Nina to express her condolences. It was an unusual thing to do, as they were not close, and Nina did not enjoy receiving visitors. On the wall hung a portrait and next to it a rectangular space where another portrait would have been. The portrait that remained was of young Liza. The missing one, her aunt said, was of Stepan, but she did not know where it had gone. Mum and Nina sat on the sofa and looked at old photos together, as would have been usual after a death of a relative. Mum noticed a stack of photos tied with a black ribbon. There was a note on top, tucked under the ribbon: 'After my death, if nobody wants these, burn them.' They were all photos of the Mardarenko-Sarazhyn clan. Mum tentatively asked if she could take them, and the portrait, too. Nina said, 'Pah, what do you need them for? OK, take them if you like.' This, to me, is illustrative of one of Ukraine's — or perhaps humanity's — divides. I find there are two extremes: people either throw their family photographs into the skip, or pack them into suitcases when fleeing from war.

Some members of our family insist that Liza was born into an impoverished family, paupered further by her husband's lavish gambling, but the portrait of her in her youth speaks of something different. It was taken in around 1910 and she looks distinguished. Her hair is pinned into an Edwardian pompadour style, and I don't think she needed to use a special hoop to make it look high at the front. Liusia often mentioned that Liza's hair was so long and thick that she would ask her children to cut huge chunks out by the roots. In this photograph, Liza wore hooped gold earrings and a neat chequered dress with a stiff collar and the image of her face — the mirror of mine — looks like a photograph, but you can see brushstrokes in her hair and clothing, where it has been manually retouched with a brush dipped in ink.

Liusia said that her mother-in-law was stern. Liza's second portrait was presumably taken after the Second World War, and you don't need to know much detail about her life to see that it had not been easy. There is no more pompadour, the hair is slicked back and looks thinner, the earrings are gone, the dress is made of thick, rough cotton with visible holes on the right shoulder, the collar looks crumpled. The shape of her face, the strong jawline and cheekbones, feel familiar. Her mouth is meatier than mine or Mum's, but the shape is similar. Her smile lines are prominent, but they don't look like they came from laughter. I used to think that the hooded eyelids and furrowed brow made her look angry, but now I see something else... but cannot figure out exactly what it is. I send the photo to the family WhatsApp group and ask: 'What do you see?' My niece, twenty-year-old Liza, named for her great-great-grandmother, replies immediately and bluntly, 'She sees a dead end, and accepts her destiny.'

In 1939, Hitler and Stalin signed a pact and invaded Poland from its western and eastern borders respectively. The Soviet newspapers were largely quiet about Poland being taken apart. However, I find a scan of a newspaper clipping, a large front-page picture of young men with shaven heads and gormless smiles. Below, it states: 'Conscription into the Red Army and the Navy takes place with great patriotic spirit.'

By the time Viktor and Liusia married in 1940, Viktor had already received his mobilisation ticket. He hadn't told Liusia, because he was worried she would call off the wedding. I guess that settles the question of who chased after whom. I call it a 'wedding', but I don't believe there was a celebration. Viktor was mobilised the following week and was promptly sent to Balashov, a town in Russia in the Saratov region, an unthinkable 1,223 kilometres north-east of Voznesensk. In June 1941, almost a year into their long-distance marriage, Liusia went to visit Viktor at his post. Mum imagined for me what their visit was like, in a series of voice notes.

'Her twentieth birthday was coming up, perhaps her visit was a gift to herself and to Dad. Her mother Yaryna would have helped her to sew a new dress. She would have helped to pack Liusia's bag, too, as it was a long journey. She would have only been able to travel there by train, and she didn't know yet that this was the beginning of a much longer and harder journey than she thought. He would have met her at the station and kissed her; she squeezed his waist. He would have asked how his mother was, but Liusia would have said she didn't know, she hadn't plucked up the courage to visit his family while he was away. Liza was cold towards Liusia, perhaps she thought Liusia was not a good enough match for her son. Viktor lived in the barracks, but I imagine he would have rented a room for Liusia in someone's house, somewhere where they could be intimate. Even though he was conscripted, they didn't know why exactly, and they don't know what's coming yet.'

Mum's voice wobbles and breaks and the voice note is interrupted. A pause, and she sends one more, voice once again composed and steady. 'After a week of her being there, the war was announced. What if Liusia did not even have a chance to say goodbye to him? Imagine the panic at those train stations! The war was coming. Were places already being bombed somewhere in Ukraine, were there reports? She would have been so worried about her life, and Vitechka's, and her family. There was no way to communicate, no phones she could have used, and it was a really long, 1,000-kilometre journey back home.'

My Uncle Viktor's notes state that on '22 June, two days before her twentieth birthday, they found out Hitler was now at war with the Soviet Union. On 23 June, Viktor and his regiment were packed into a train and sent towards the western borders of Ukraine. The result of this visit was me.' Liusia, who didn't yet know that she was carrying her first child, returned on another train to Voznesensk. She would call her first boy Viktor, and now finally I understand why we kept picking the same names over and over in our family. By the time Viktor Jr was born nine months later, Liusia was living under German-Romanian occupation and assumed her husband was dead.

A huge army of 600,000 Soviet soldiers, many of them Ukrainian, fought in the battle of Kyiv in 1941. Viktor Sr, my grandfather, was among them. At the end of September, in the so-called 'Kyiv Encirclement', Viktor was hiding in the reeds of the Dnipro River. The weather was unusually cold, and, in the early hours of the morning, the water was covered with a thin sheet of ice. When German soldiers came by, they would blindly shoot at the water. Viktor could not swim, and, up to his waist in the icy river, he would duck into it when the rat-at-at-at-at came. He was eventually captured by the Germans, along with more than 400,000 Soviet soldiers, and taken to a filtration camp in Germany. Many died from hunger, or were executed, but Victor had specialist skills — he was a driver, mechanic and locksmith — and, perhaps because of these, he survived. He was selected as a driver for the family of a military superior who was at the front. His job was to take the VIP's wife to the shops, or his children to school, ferrying things and people here and there.

'But this lasted only until the Germans realised that they might have to retreat and began to build the so-called "eastern rampart",' my uncle's notes say. His father was then sent to the Ostwall tunnel construction site. It was here he met someone called Vasyl Romanovsky, from Besarabia, and together they hatched a plan to escape. Southern Ukraine up to the South Buh River was occupied by the Romanians (who were on the side of the Germans), and Voznesensk, where Liusia lived, was occupied by the Germans, so it was risky for Viktor to turn up there. He and Vasyl lay low in Besarabia, working for a farmer and hiding in the corn fields if the Romanian military were seen nearby.

Liusia often mentioned two stories from that time, dark stories that always play out like a black-and-white movie in my imagination. In one of them, Liusia said she saw people in a line being taken somewhere. She thought it was a deportation, because it looked very similar to when the Soviets took her to the cattle train in 1931. She must have remembered what it was like and so she threw a crust of bread into the line of people. She was chased by an armed soldier, but ran into the house and was hidden in peryna (a stack of down winter blankets) by her mother Yaryna. In the second story, she ends up in the line herself, and by now she knows it is not a line for deportation. From 29 to 30 September, approximately 34,000 of Kyiv's Jews were rounded up and systematically marched to a ravine outside the city, called Babi Yar, where they were shot, in one of the largest Nazi massacres of the Second World War. Similar scenarios were happening in other cities and towns, including Voznesensk, which had a large Jewish community. Liusia was dragged into the line with her baby son, who already had a full head of curly black hair, to shouts of 'Yude. Yude.' This time she grabbed the arm of a Romanian gendarme and squeezed out a sentence in Romanian; thanks to the half-Moldovan Yaryna, it was her mother's tongue. She pleaded that she was Moldovan, and he let her out of the line.

In the three years of their occupation, there was no freedom of movement within the areas occupied by the Germans. There was a curfew too, and people were not allowed to leave their own area unless they had special permission. I wonder if the Romanians were more lenient, especially towards those who spoke their language. I have no idea how, but Liusia and her baby son Viktor made it to Besarabia and were reunited with Viktor. They conceived another child, my Aunt Yevheniia.

However, once the Germans and Romanians were pushed out of the USSR by the Red Army in 1944, Viktor left once again to rejoin the Third Ukrainian Front's anti-tank regiment, where he remained for the rest of the war. There was a great shortage of vehicles within the Soviet Army, but a lend-lease programme (USA aid to its allies) was extended to the USSR and the Americans sent an estimated 200,000 Studebaker trucks. Viktor was assigned a Studebaker-US6, an armoured vehicle used for towing artillery and transporting soldiers and provisions. The Soviets called the vehicles 'Studer' and they were billed as the Soviets' 'victory trucks'. Viktor managed the millipede gun, dragged around by the Studer. He received about ten Soviet medals, among them the 'medal for courage', 'medal for the capture of Cisinau', 'medal for the capture of Budapest', 'medal for the capture of Vienna' and 'Order of Victory'. But he loathed what he went through. He often said to his children, 'All the real heroes fell on the first days of the war, we just tried to survive.' And he never wore his medals, not even to skip the queues of the Brezhnev era.

I remember Uncle Viktor mentioning Vienna in one of my recordings, and go back to them to re-listen.

Viktor's rusty voice hisses into my phone loudly, 'Father was scared to talk about the war. But one thing he did mention was how much he hated ofitseryo' (a diminutive, an offensive nickname for officers or military commanders). 'They were all balalayshyky [Russians]. The Soviet Second and Third Ukrainian Fronts went back through Vienna after the war finished. The shop windows in Vienna were not like in the USSR…' He is interrupted by his brother Slava, 'Yes, they'd never even seen such beauty in that shithole of theirs!' Viktor continues, 'There were delicate, large mirrors, ornate, gilded, beautiful. But the officers would order the men to go by-by-by-by-by-by-by with a machine gun. Just blow it all up, just to destroy. And then they looted, they were mainly after the alcohol, then clothes, food.' Slava concurs in a severe voice, 'Yes, and chocolate!' 'Father hated that. Why shoot up the show-windows, what was the point? Just to destroy, just to destroy. But when he was telling us this, he was cautious, he said this quietly.'

The tragedies of those years were so relentless, you'd think it was made up. Following the war there was another famine. The weather was too dry in 1946–47. The winter had been dry, and so was the following spring and summer. It was as if all the moisture in this part of the world was gone, evaporated from the earth through blood and tears. The harvests were meagre in the regions of Kherson, Mykolayiv and Besarabia, where Liusia, Viktor and their two children settled down after Viktor's demobilisation, way below what Stalin's Five-Year Plan required. All the stored grain was requisitioned by the Soviet government, just as it had been during the Holodomor in the 1930s. This grain was exported to help feed the western edges of the Soviet Empire, such as Yugoslavia and Czechoslovakia, or sent to be stored in special silos in the Urals. In addition, the Soviets introduced a tax on trees, fruit-bearing shrubs and animals. So, if you owned fruit trees, berry bushes or farm animals, you were supposed to pay an unfathomable amount of money in tax for each. As people did not have this money, it would have been taken out of their trudoden (wage). Therefore you took an axe to the tree, and to the pig, too. Thousands of fruit and walnut trees, as well as pigs, goats, cows and birds, were destroyed by the struggling peasants.

It is estimated that up to a million people died as the result of this famine. There were over a million more reported to have dystrophy.

In the online regional archives, I stumble upon a letter written by Zhadan NK, from Yasenka village to a relative in Odesa. You can almost hear the exhaustion in the woman's words. '... Kostya, we live now as if encased in a black coffin, just trying to survive, we don't know what to do or where to go. The children have no clothes. We went to the head of kolkhoz [the collective farm] for help, but they laugh at us, because they are not hungry. We earned 1,000 trudoden at kolkhoz, but they don't give us anything in return, we starve like dogs.'

This tax was so crushing because your animals, and the things you grew in your garden, were a lifeline for people in the villages. Owning a cow was a dream to a lot of villagers at the time, as having enough resources to feed it was not an easy task, even in times of relative stability. All the pastures and meadows belonged to the state-owned collective farms and it was forbidden to take your own animal to pasture there. Queues for fodder were impossibly long. In 1947, if you managed to keep your cow alive and to hide your grain, you lived. I ask Mum how they could afford to keep a cow with such a high tax, and she replies that there was an option to pay in milk. In another letter I find, a contemporary from Mykolayiv says simply, 'You ate if you stole.' Liusia's stories confirmed this.

She often told us a story about korzhyky, the simple flatbreads that she made using a bit of whey and flour. She would fry them in the morning and pack them for Viktor to take with him to work (he had found a job as a truck driver for a motor depot after the war). She noticed that he was losing weight and looked weaker, until he came back home one day and dropped on the floor. He confessed that he did not eat any of his lunch, he gave it to the women and children starving on the streets. Another time, as she sat at the kitchen table with her children, a man with a crazed look in his eyes ran in, grabbed their flatbreads and scarpered.

Liusia gave birth to their third child, Valentina, in February 1947, and to their fourth, Slava, in September 1948. The famine was over, but Viktor's wage was not enough to feed a family of six plus their cow. One summer day, Viktor was driving his truck and stopped by the side of the road next to a wheat field. The thin strip of the kerb was a motley mass of pale purple and dusty green, what they called sudanka (sorghum, or Sudanese grass) and shchyrytsa (wild amaranth). He always had a small scythe tucked at the back of the truck. He cut off a heap and dropped it in his yard at home, for the cow to eat. Someone must have seen him, because the news of Viktor ravaging the Communist meadows travelled fast. Soon enough, a policeman showed up at the gate. The Law of Five Spikelets had been introduced in 1932, a harbinger of Holodomor. This law implied that taking just five spikelets (ears of wheat) from a field would result in severe punishment: dispossession, prison, sometimes execution. By 1949, when Viktor took food for the cow, this law had been slightly softened. A death sentence no longer applied, but still, '… theft, misappropriation, embezzlement or other theft of collective farm, cooperative or other public property is punishable by imprisonment in a forced labour camp for a term of five to eight years with or without confiscation of property.' Viktor was given the maximum eight years of forced labour in a gulag.

The cruelty of the punishment wasn't just to do with the length of time that he had to serve, but also the location, or rather, the distance. Viktor was not just locked away in a prison in Ukraine, or on the Russian border, he was sent to the other side of the world, 11,000 kilometres away, to a labour camp on the island of Sakhalin, its southern tip a boat ride away from

Northern Japan. There was no way to visit him, and no way to contact him either. Liusia wrote to all the authorities she could think of. She even sent some of Viktor's war medals to prove that he was a good man, but she never got a response and the medals were never returned. Viktor was sent to Sakhalin to begin the construction of the Sakhalin Tunnel, a monumental project which aimed to join the island with mainland Russia under the Nevelskoy Strait. In winter, Viktor was to drive the truck with materials across the frozen strait. Once, the ice cracked underneath the weight of the truck, sucking it under, and yet again Viktor, who still couldn't swim, found himself struggling to get out of icy waters.

My grandfather rarely mentioned any other details about his time there, apart from the fact that every day in the labour camp was fraught with danger… and the main danger, more often than not, came from fellow inmates. In Russian, the word bespredel literally means 'without limits', and figuratively means 'lawlessness'. Apart from political prisoners and people like my grandfather, the labour camps were full of bespredelshchiks, 'the lawless'. Surviving the tough hours of forced labour as well as malnutrition and being apart from your family was only half the battle: the other half was avoiding being murdered.

There is a photo of Liusia and her four children, taken a few months after Viktor was arrested, sitting in a photo atelier with the typical backdrop of birch trees. I asked Mum why Liusia had a formal photograph taken during such lean, hungry times when money and food were so short. 'Do you notice how thin Liusia looks,' Mum replied. 'She was starving. The picture was taken in 1947 or 1948, during Holodomor, when all the available food would have gone to her four children. Liusia said she felt so ill and emaciated that at one point she thought she was dying. She arranged for this photo to be taken so that if she died, her children would have something to remember her by.'

Liusia and the children would have starved had Viktor's mother Liza not summoned them back to Voznesensk, where she lived with her son Volodymyr and his family. The way Liusia remembers Liza is not flattering. Liza used to tell Liusia, 'Why are you having children every year, like a rabbit? How will you feed them all, give them a decent life?' As if only Liusia was complicit in those births. With so much trauma and death, Liusia and Viktor must have wanted to keep creating life and I understand that desire completely. But after her son was imprisoned, Liza couldn't leave Liusia alone with a baby and three other children. She housed them in her summer kitchen, where they stayed until 1953.

On 5 March 1953, Stalin croaked. And this is the only word my family, and millions of others, would ever use to describe his death. In whispers, 'Oora, Stalin sdokh!' ('Hurrah, Stalin croaked!') Death was too noble a word for that man. Little did they know, but he did literally croak. In her description of his last moments, his daughter Svetlana Alliluyeva says (my translation): 'The agony was terrifying. Death choked him right in front of our eyes. At some point – and I am not sure this is true, but this is how it seemed – he opened his eyes and cast a glance at everyone who stood around him. It was a terrifying glance, insane or furious, full of fear of death.'

The radio was on that morning. Volodymyr was inside, listening. First came the Soviet anthem, then ghostly, sombre bells. Then, the chief Soviet radio announcer, 'the voice of the Soviet Union', Yuri Levitan. His tragic broadcasting voice announced, 'Govorit Moskva' ('Moscow speaking'). 'Dear comrades and friends, the Central Committee of the Communist Party, the Council of Ministers and the Presidium of the Supreme Soviet of the USSR announce with deep grief to the party and workers that on 5 March at 9:50 in the evening, Iosif Vissarionovich Stalin, Secretary of the Central Committee of the Communist Party and Chairman of the Council of Ministers, died after a serious illness. The heart of the genius companion and follower of Lenin's work, the wise leader and teacher of the Communist party and of the Soviet people, stopped beating.' (Again, this is my translation.) He continues with the declaration that, in these dark days, peoples all over their beautiful, huge country will unite even more strongly in the great brotherly family led by the Communist Party.

Liusia was in her mother-in-law's garden. She saw Volodymyr running towards her; he squeezed her hands tight and hissed, 'Liusia! Stalin croaked! Maybe Vitechka will be let out of prison soon.' Then they heard Volodymyr's wife Lyolka's genuine wailing and lamentations... and, for the first time, they play-acted together a motion that is repeated by anyone who tells this story up to this day: they wet their eyes with their spit, in case Lyolka would be inclined to denounce them for not feeling sadness for the great leader's death.

Lavrentiy Beria, the NKVD chief nicknamed Stalin's 'Shadow Cardinal', introduced an amnesty that reached far and wide. Liusia often said that, even though this was good news for Viktor, there was a detail that also made it dangerous. Beria ordered the release of urki, hardened criminals, at the same time as the political prisoners. This way a lot of the political prisoners would be dealt with by the urki and the bonus effect would be to sow chaos. Chaos among the population meant another opportunity to repress and control. Beria was soon shot through the forehead by General Pavel Batitsky, but his amnesty went ahead anyway and had the desired effect. Everyone was released at once. People like my grandfather were let out of the labour camps alongside genuine thieves and murderers and sent back into mainland Russia and beyond on freight trains, together. The criminals organised themselves into gangs. They murdered on the trains, they robbed and killed people in the villages. Viktor and a friend jumped off the train they were put on almost immediately. They hid in the forest and waited until the trains carrying the criminals had all left.

Viktor rejoined Liusia in Voznesensk later in 1953, that year of Stalin's death, and started building a house, adjacent to his brother Volodymyr's. And they had more children, Yura in 1954 and my mother Olga in 1958. Viktor found a job as a truck driver for a cattle veterinarian. He was only paid 70 rubles a month. Without fail, my family explains the salary's worth in terms of garments. 'Olechkaaaaa, a decent suit cost around 140 rubles, can you imagine?! Try feeding a family of eight with this money and living with dignity!' The tree and animal tax was abolished a year after Stalin's death, so the family were pretty much self-sufficient in terms of food supply, but other necessities and luxuries, such as well-tailored suits, were financially beyond their reach.

There was a system by means of which you could apply for a bigger apartment or even a car, but it took an average of fifteen to twenty years to receive what you were waiting for. Liusia felt that being zhduny – one of the 'waiting' – was not for her. She wanted her children to have the best education and the best possible clothes, in spite of their limited circumstances. She could not work full-time; there were too many children to look after and soon enough her eldest children had children of their own, too. There was no opportunity to find what we now call freelance work, or even part-time work. And there were no banks, or any loans you could take out. So when the youngest children were old enough to go to school, she began to run her own tiny underground business.

Most kinds of personal trade were prohibited in the Soviet Union. You were assigned a job by the government and that was that. Any kind of dealing was called spekulyatziya and was punishable by law. But there were different types of spekulants: the swindlers and the covert traders. For example, when my parents were university students, you would hear a quick 'psssst' in the public toilets, and a shady spekulant would quickly flash you a pair of jeans from their bag. They would demand the money up front and right away, because they could be busted at any time. You would hurriedly dish out the money, take the bag with the much-demanded foreign jeans… and inside find one lonely trouser leg.

And then there was Liusia.

Along the long, lonely roads of Ukraine's flat steppe, trees were being planted en masse. After the devastating effect of the tree tax, another policy had come in, that of nature 'melioration'. Fruit trees were now being planted in an attempt to stop soil erosion and to protect the collectivised farm fields (collectivisation was not going well, by the way). Wild apricots still bloom today between the roads and the fields and produce small, pockmarked fruit.

Liusia saw an opportunity. In the dead of night, she scoured the roads, picking apricots or cherries, kilos and kilos of fruit. The next day, again in the small hours of the morning, so as not to be denounced by a neighbour she didn't get on with, Viktor would drive her to the train station. There – if she was lucky, as it was impossible to reserve a ticket – she would buy a ticket for Moscow or St Petersburg, where she would sell the fruit. She did it, she explained, *v try oborota*, a figure-skating term meaning *in three turns*. She would get to Kazan, where her sister Lida lived, and sell the apricots or cherries there. Then she would buy something in Kazan and take it to Moscow to sell. Then she would buy something in Moscow and finally shift it in Voznesensk.

Mum remembers accompanying Liusia and being bought a black fur coat and tall white boots that glistened in the winter light. They were so unusual and precious, Mum remembers she couldn't stop staring down at them while walking to school with her brother Yura; there were none like that in the whole of Voznesensk. Yura, who was four years older than Mum, was her best friend. But this time he called her *gadina*, 'a toad', and threatened to leave her behind if she didn't stop staring at her new boots.

In the 'family summit' voice recording from August 2021, the extreme lengths of Liusia's hustle were revealed. The voices shriek at the excitement of remembering this story and interrupt each other constantly. But I manage to piece together the following.

Once, she travelled with a friend 5,000 kilometres to Vorkuta, the home of one of the largest gulags, called Vorkutlag, with 3,000 eggs. Three thousand eggs! How on earth do you transport 3,000 eggs across thousands of kilometres? But she allegedly did. Two huge woven baskets, with half the eggs in cartons and sewn in place with flower-patterned cloth to stop them from moving and breaking. The other half were packed into a heavy, angular suitcase made out of cardboard, normally used for ripening pears.

The baskets were extremely heavy. During the conversation, I frantically try to calculate how heavy those baskets were. I shout, '171 kilos! Plus the weight of the baskets! Are you sure it was just two women? How could they have managed? Maybe it was 2,000 eggs, that seems more doable, you lot love to exaggerate!' The whole operation took them a week. Liusia brought back 130 rubles, almost twice Viktor's monthly wage.

The story continues. Liusia was tall and voluptuous and her friend Verka was short and voluptuous. Everyone in Vorkuta was skinny and draped in furs. After they had finished trading, Liusia and Verka would go to the market to buy ingredients to cook back at their bedsit. On one of those days, there was something that resembled lamb meat for sale. Everyone in the queue was asking for 200 grams of meat. Liusia took a kilo. She heard people whisper, in a way that I can still hear coming out of Aunt Liuda's mouth when she told the story, 'Aaaaani balniye' ('These women are crazy'). Liusia retorted back loudly to the whispers, 'How can you all be dressed in furs, but spend so little on food? You are the crazy ones!'

In the times when she wasn't hauling heavy baskets of fruit or eggs, travelling for weeks to the edges of the Soviet Empire and back, Liusia did a lot of physical work at home. Say it was summer, Liusia would rise at 4 a.m., before dawn. The cow was in the dugout barn beside the summer kitchen, waiting to be fed. Liusia would chop some beetroot and mix it with some hay, or chop pumpkins (for the best, yellowest butter), or mix in a whole bunch of 'oil cakes', milled sunflower husks. She would then milk the cow, called Maia (it feels as though all her cows throughout her life had the same name!), and take her to the neighbour, who collected other cows on the street and, for a small fee, would take them out to pasture. The sleeves of the Arbuzinka River were embroidered with neat stitches of branching paths and small bridges. Red squirrels jumped over the crowns of 150-year-old oaks. Grey herons with their orange beaks and dark feathered toque hats, like a million huge typewriters, would sing takakakaka. More oaks, ash trees, maples, alders. There, among the trees, the cows pastured.

Liusia would return home to feed the chickens and pigs and then prepare the produce to take on one of her epic trips to sell at the market. She would walk back to the pasture (a distance of four or five kilometres) with a bucket of extra food for the cow, so the cow would not move or kick while she milked her. If small children were around, either her own youngest – Yura and my mum — or her eldest children's children, they would be taken along to swat the huge horseflies that buzzed around the cow while she was milked. Liusia would carry the heavy bucket of milk back home and distribute it among the three-litre jars left on a bench by her front gate. Her neighbours bought the milk, still warm.

Education was paramount, especially because the family did not live in a big city and so had fewer resources or opportunities; besides that they were beyond the reach of the influential and powerful who could be bribed for a university place. Liusia herself had a quick and curious mind; she had received a very basic education — a bit of arithmetic and how to read and write — but she read voraciously. Like everything, books were in great deficit and there were always big queues for certain books at the library. If you finally got to borrow a sought-after book, it had to be returned very quickly, after a maximum of three days. The most-wanted books weren't even allowed to leave the library, instead, they had to be read in the reading room. Uncle Viktor would spend two days reading the books he could take home after school. Then it was his mother Liusia's turn. She would have just one day, or rather one night, to crunch through Mayne Reid's *The Headless Horseman*, *The Lady of the Camellias* by Alexandre Dumas, or Victor Hugo's *The Man Who Laughs*. She would start reading a book after finishing all the chores at 9 p.m. and finish it by 3 a.m. One hour's kip and then she was up again, to milk the cow.

Liusia often teased her husband, who supposedly came from a more refined family, by telling guests, 'He's only read two books his whole life! *The White Birch*' (about the Second World War) 'and *Alitet Goes to the Hills*' (an anti-American propaganda novel about the indigenous people of Chukotka). Viktor would smile and retort, 'I have read three books, Maty [Mother], you forget *Korolenko in Bad Company*!' And Liusia would retort, 'Korolenko was the name of the author, Vitechka, not part of the title!' Most often, Viktor called Liusia the Ukrainian 'Maty'. She had two names for him. 'Vitechka' was for when everything was fine and 'Viktor' for when he did something wrong. She could be harsh, especially when it came to drinking. She could tell from the angle of his silhouette on the hill if he had been drinking, and would be ready with thunder and lightning: 'Viktor, do not give me the nerves!' Too many veterans became alcoholics, but not on her watch; that was just not an option for Viktor.

Viktor died when he was eighty-five. I was twelve. In Ukraine, you don't mess around; someone dies and pretty much the next day they are buried. I remember going to the house and there he was, in an open casket, face taut and ashen. It was a shock to see him dead, I groan-cried, and Uncle Viktor told me to pull myself together. The funeral procession went through the village slowly, dragging with it the long, deep wails of the brass band. At the cemetery, my mum tried to throw her body on top of the now-closed coffin when they started lowering it in. I'd never seen her in so much pain before.

After Viktor died, Liusia's health suddenly worsened. It became too hard to take care of her house and the smallholding in the village by herself. My parents bought her the flat in Kakhovka, where she lived for the next six years. Mum says Liusia was only bedbound for a couple of weeks. She managed to get up for her eighty-fourth birthday on 24 June. She didn't dress up, but she did fix her hair. Mum and Aunt Liuda brought some food round, and they sat at the small square table by the kitchen window and had a glass of fizz. Liusia became quieter after her birthday. For two weeks, she would put her chin on the palm of her hand and she would sing an old melancholy song, a song Mum didn't know and had never heard Liusia sing before. Unlike Stalin, Liusia was not scared of death. She used to say, 'If I am, death cannot be. When death will come, I will no longer be here. So we will never meet face to face. I have nothing to fear.'

I was twenty when Liusia died. I was in Sicily, on a year abroad improving my Italian, which I studied at the University of Warwick. It makes me feel good now to realise that Liusia knew that one of her descendants attended a university in England; perhaps she felt it was a mission accomplished. But though I try not to regret anything in life, I do regret not flying back for the funeral. I regret not being there for my mum, who took Liusia's death even harder than her father's.

Liusia said once that if she was given a chance to live her whole life again, and if there was no other way but to repeat it exactly as it was, she would do it. She would live her life once more, she would endure the horrors again, if only she also had the chance to live through all the good moments, too. She loved life so fiercely. She sang life into her flowers, and into us, but that last song of hers was different. She knew it was time to go. Liusia never did look death in the face; she died peacefully in her sleep.

There have been times since 2022 when I have felt as though it would never be possible to feel joy like we did before the war. There have been times when I thought, never will I be able to let go completely when I play with my children, never will I enjoy the moment truly, never will I be able to forget about chaos and cruelty and death. But Liusia sang to her flowers and watered her children in a way that seeped down to the following generation. She was unique, and she was also like millions of other Ukrainian women of her generation: with straight backs and reverence for life, not death.

During the week after Liusia's death, my mum and I had very similar dreams. In my dream I am up in the sky. The clouds are voluminous and bulbous, like the huge heads of half-opened peonies. I see a massive building, not unlike a Krushchev-era block of flats, but truly enormous, colossal even. I am on the top floor, in my Aunt Zhenia's kitchen. The light is pouring in through the window and the table is illuminated. Zhenia's favourite snacks are laid out on little plates: black tea with lemon, slices of white bread and some cheese. The blue bowl with golden details is full of buckwheat honey. Zhenia used to love to put the salty cheese on bread and drizzle over the honey. Out of the window I see Liusia; she is riding a bike with an oversized basket attached to the front: how European, Parisian even! In the basket she has bunches of radishes, some ridged powder-pink tomatoes, a classic rectangular loaf of bread which was called 'the brick', some more cheese.

Anxious that she is living in a flat again, with no outside space and no garden, I ask her, 'Are you happy?' She says yes, everyone lives in one enormous building, and the people are friendly, the market is great. I think, 'Ha, I knew it, this proletarian dream house is only possible in an alternative reality, in dreams or in heaven or both.' Then Liusia says, with relief, 'I just look after the house, but Vitechka found a job. He fixes satellites!'

I rush to tell my mum the dream. 'I too had this dream,' she says. 'Not the house in the sky, but that Tato was fixing "antennas".' We both feel better and choose to believe that they both stay in touch with us, thanks to my grandfather tinkering with God's satellites.

Vera Paskova, Tashkent, Uzbekistan, circa 1956

4

The Night Beauty

In February 2014, Russia invaded Crimea, the southern region of Ukraine. Five months later, I set off for home – along with my photographer Kris – to work on my first cookbook. People I met in the UK often put Eastern European food into one basket – potatoes, dumplings, overcooked cabbage – and with good reason. There had been the equivalent of Russification, or rather Sovietisation, in the world of Eastern Europe's eating and cooking, something that was called 'standardisation'. Industrialisation in the Soviet Union meant that food was mass-produced. Those in urban centres often lived in communal flats that were ill-equipped for any meaningful, let alone soulful, cooking; people were strongly encouraged to – or sometimes had no choice but to – eat in the Soviet communal eating areas, where the food was dreadful. The cooks were required to put strictly standardised amounts of every ingredient into the dishes, which were all bad 'economic' recipes to begin with, made with poor-quality produce.

A distinctly Soviet cuisine emerged, too, with dishes like the mayo-slathered olivye, 'Russian salad', being the most ubiquitous. There was not one New Year table without a two-litre bowl filled with olivye. In the canteens, there was a standard recipe for each 'national' dish of the larger Soviet countries. A regulation kharcho from Georgia, borsch from Ukraine, plov from Central Asia.

At home, however, especially in the countryside, where people were able to grow their own produce and keep an animal or two, good food had survived and I wanted to celebrate this kind of cooking. I wanted to show my readers regional South Ukrainian cooking, as seen through the lens of my family. I wanted to reclaim its colour and regional identity. I wanted there to be photographs from the market, with mountains of soft herbs – dill and coriander and purple basil – huge tomatoes and pink beetroots with their handwritten signs proclaiming borscheviy buriak, 'beetroot for borsch'.

Before Kris and I had been allowed into the country, we'd had to sign a disclaimer that we knew and accepted the risk of going into a war zone. First we went to Kyiv, to record my Ukrainian-Armenian aunt's recipes, then we took the twelve-hour sleeper train to Kherson, then to Kakhovka, to record the dishes of the town of Tavriya and my mum's recipes, and then finally by car to Voznesensk, to visit my paternal grandmother Vera, my last surviving grandparent. Vera opened the clunky old gate to us with huge lacquered hair, wearing a frilly organza top I'd never seen before. I froze. Not even a hello.

'Babushka! What's up with you?' 'What?' 'What are you wearing? Why is your hair like this?' She looked startled, and suddenly sad. 'The neighbour came and did my hair. What about the foto sessiya?' 'Yes, exactly, it's happening! I need you to be natural, Grandma! Your purple khalat, go put that on, please! Bozh!' Defeated and disorientated by my demands, she changed into the robe dress she always wore in the summer and combed her hair back down.

Vera loved having her photograph taken in general. When she was younger, she posed proudly, always wearing a dark red lipstick to accentuate the rounded bow of her lips, hair made up and perfect, in patterned or colourful dresses. She loved looking good. She came up with special nicknames for us. She was the Night Beauty, Mum was the Day Beauty and I was the Morning Beauty, the times of the day chosen to indicate our ages. She wanted us to know that we were all beautiful, at all stages, forever.

Kris and I drove into the yard, into the shadow of the grapevines, Vera's little guard dog, a mutt, barking. Voznesensk is a town, but it has a village feel when you visit a house like Vera's. The cockerels are shouting and there are clanging noises from the sunflower oil factory right opposite her gates. Billions of tiny little oil droplets float through the air and burst inside your nostrils, smelling of toasted sunflower seeds which have just been crushed.

   I regretted having been so anxious on arrival and I was relieved to see Vera emerge in a good mood. She tells me how good-looking the photographer is, that smile! She beams back at him. The flower-patterned, purple day dress with dusty pink hems, buttoned at the front, is like her uniform. In the photographs Kris took, she looks happy, a wide smile with a row of neat dentures. She'd already prepped the dough for the dumplings and she'd cooked a huge stack of pancakes, her speciality. Kris sees the tiny kitchen she works from and exclaims, 'How is it possible to produce banquet quantities of food from such a small space!?'

Vera's house was very particular. Built from scratch by my grandfather, Vera's second husband, it was made traditionally out of bricks moulded from local clay and straw. The ceilings were very low, which meant that the windows outside lay low too. For years, the toilet was outside, until my dad built an annexe room with an inside toilet. The house had two entrances after that: the original kitchenette entrance by the summer kitchen, and this second, unconventional door, where you enter right into the toilet, before passing through into the narrow living room.

The living room was also the guest room and the dining room, too. When guests arrived, a long, narrow Formica table was brought in and plonked in front of the sofa. Rickety chairs would be lined up along the other side and Vera would keep shuffling to and fro. She wanted to see us eat, and she wanted us to groan from being full. Like Liusia and so many women of her generation, she was a compulsive feeder. She was a good cook, not as natural as Liusia, but she had a number of dishes in her repertoire that she knew well and executed perfectly. We called them her 'greatest hits', one of them being beshparmak, a four-ingredient Central Asian dish that she had adapted to suit her local ingredients, or more specifically swapped lamb and lamb fat for chicken and chicken fat. All you needed was eggs, flour and water to make diamond-shaped pasta, a really good chicken that used to run but also had a nice layer of fat, and some onions. You poached the chicken in salted water, skimmed the chicken fat and cooked the onions in it until caramelised; you then cooked the pasta in the chicken broth and finally you layered chicken, onions and pasta into a mountain of what I can only call heaven on Earth.

The door to the kitchenette was permanently open in the summer, covered by a white lace curtain. Behind it, a snug, dark cool space, two metres square at most. There was a tiny hob and a tubby, noisy Soviet fridge. And then there was another room, windowless, so even darker and snugger, with a specific smell of flour and pickles. There was a masonry oven to the right and mocha-coloured patterned wallpaper. A great big dresser leaned against the wall, with glasses and china stacked at the top and two big drawers below, where the flour was kept. Finally, there was la pièce de résistance – at least to me, I am not sure she felt it was extraordinary – a table with a special insert that you could pull out, like a pull-out desk. This is where Vera rolled out the pasta dough and shaped either varenyky filled with curd cheese or meat-filled pelmeni dumplings, my brother's favourite. The pelmeni dumplings never made it into the book, even though every Ukrainian makes and loves them. Things felt so raw at that time. I deemed them 'too Russian' and banned them from the manuscript. How were Vera's dumplings responsible for the war? I could not rationally explain, but they felt complicit.

Vera, you see, was Russian. She was born in Siberia in 1928 and lived there for the first two decades of her life. When I started writing this chapter, I wanted to explore what her Russian-ness meant. How could I make sense of it, now that everything had changed irreversibly?

I realised that Vera never talked about where she was from. As far as I know, she had never gone back to Siberia to see her family; she didn't ever tell us stories and she had no relatives around, apart from her daughter Valia, my dad's (half) sister, to bring any stories to life. One thing she used to say was that she was cheldonka. I used to quiz her about it, but even though she identified as cheldonka, she didn't have much to add; she simply said it meant chelovek s Dona, a man from the Don River. I did some digging later on and found out that the Cheldon people may have been the first colonial settlers in Siberia, arriving as early as the fifteenth century (some of them from areas very close to modern Ukraine's borders) and possibly mixing with indigenous Siberian tribes. My research did shed light on the way Vera spoke. We often teased her about the way she talked; it was a distinctive Siberian dialect. She dragged her vowels and shortened endings of Russian verbs, saying, for instance, kaka instead of kakaya, or taka instead of takaya.

I had only ever been to Russia twice, both times to Moscow to visit my uncle, and the experience did not reveal much. But Siberia was a different place completely. It was huge, it was far away, and in my mind it was wrapped in a milky film, as if on the other side of frosted privacy glass. I asked Vera to open that window and to tell me about her life.

In summer 2015, I was staying with my parents in Kakhovka and Vera came to visit us. It was an opportunity to get her away from her potatoes and incessant cooking and preserving, a week for her to relax and really enjoy us all. I still have a stack of photos from that visit, which we took all over the garden. By that point, I was already a fan of a nonchalant natural artsy photography, but my family didn't get it. We all absolutely had to pose together, looking straight at the camera, against a background of blooming flowers or some kind of greenery. It seemed so important to them. In all the photos, Vera is wearing a wide-brimmed hat, sometimes smiling, but mostly serious. This was a serious business. Here she is holding hands with Mum by the giant hibiscus, its petal span as wide as her hat; then with their arms hooked one in the other in the shade by the pine trees, my arm around her shoulder on a padded swing seat, the pond sparkling through long reeds. The Three Graces. Morning, Day and Night.

That year, my dad had given me a small, hand-held video camera, I think specifically for this task. I wanted to record Vera's story. It was time. We were in a silly kind of mood after the photo session in the garden, me teasing them, them waving their hands at me, demanding I put some lipstick on my contour-less bare face. We sat in the dining room, a light-filled orangery, big enough to fit a table for eight and an old Soviet cabinet that my mum had découpaged to make it look shabby-chic French. On the white-painted shelving unit, behind the extendable table covered with an embroidered white tablecloth, lived Mum's orchids, ferns, cookbooks and her small collection of English Victorian jugs and soup tureens.

Vera disappeared for five minutes and came back with refreshed brick-red lips and fluffier, taller hair.

This time I knew to back off. She sat straight and her face became very serious, like in the photos. Vera had always been communicative, even balakucha ('garrulous'), as my dad used to call her in Ukrainian. She loved to talk. At the market, in a queue, she would start a conversation and make friends. I braced myself for a riveting, fast-paced, animated story. But that's not what happened. She sat in her seat, very straight-backed. And then out of her stiff body came a stiff voice. It was almost unemotional, as if she was reading from a script. I was perplexed and kept pushing for more details, more memories. And then she began to cry. I understood that her stiffness was a barrier, a barrier against the past, perhaps to shield her from things she might have never discussed before.

I lost the tape that very year. I moved house, I was separating from my son Sasha's dad and the move was stressful. I lost the tape and also Sasha's first lock of hair and his mummified umbilical cord. I berated myself bitterly afterwards for being disorganised and careless. I had lost all the treasures. In the following years, I asked Vera questions every now and then. There was one last sit-down interview, though, in 2018, when she was suddenly very frail. It was the year before she died. It is again us three, Vera's three beauties. Mum sits opposite me, Vera to the left. The table is covered with a mottled oilcloth. There is no lipstick this time, her hair is flat and very thin. I stare at her little porcelain figurines inside the glass cabinet.

A tiny matador and a bull, and a couple – a coy young Ukrainian woman in traditional clothing, a wreath and ribbons, and a young man, cajoling her – a wooing scene. I am sure about 80 per cent of grandparents' houses in Ukraine had one just the same. Her voice is so faint, I struggle to understand what she is saying. She keeps mixing up the dates, and Mum acts as a storytelling assistant. 'Are you sure it was that year, Mama? Mama, was Petichka already born?' I skip questions when she starts crying again. It is too much, and unfair. Some questions will just have to remain unanswered forever.

Siberia has always had connotations of danger for me. When, as a child, I listened to my maternal grandmother Liusia's stories, I didn't understand where Vologda was, so I imagined Liusia had been deported to Siberia. Of course, so many were deported to Siberia, it was the place for deportations. My vision of it was mainly based on a Soviet drama called *A Station for Two*, the opening subtitles for which could have read something like, 'Somewhere in Siberia, in a corrective penal colony...' But what was it like to live there, if you were of the place?

Vera was born in Maslyanskaya, in the Tyumen region of Siberia, in September 1928. Maslyanskaya comes from the word maslo, which means 'butter' or 'oil'. I lean towards the butter definition, as for her whole life, Vera's mother Olena ended up processing milk, by the end drying caesium into a material to be used to produce items such as hair combs. Vera was one of four children. There was Valia, born two years before Vera, and Klavdiya, born two years after. Years later, in 1938, they will be joined by the baby of the family, Vladimir.

Vera said Maslyanskaya wasn't even a village, but a stantsiya, a 'train stop'. In my head, I sketched a small train station, and, further in, a cluster of wooden houses with no fences, away from civilisation and white with snow. Her father, Vasilii, was a cobbler and they got by. The money Vasilii made fixing and sewing shoes gave them a roof over their heads and allowed them to keep a cow. Still, Siberia during the civil war was turbulent. The Reds fought the Whites, and there were also British, American, Japanese and Czech troops. It was a kaleidoscope of fighting, deprivation and power-switching, until the Bolsheviks finally cemented control over the area in 1922.

I presume that, like Moisei, Vasilii was allowed to run his trade during the NEP years, but then things changed. Those who refused to join the factories or kolkhoz often became victims of summary executions. Vera said the Bolsheviks came to their house when she was four or five, in the early 1930s. They rounded up the family and took her father away. Her voice was steady until this point, but then her eyes filled and there was a silence.

'Babushka, what about your dad, did you see him again?' 'No, they shot him, I think. Then they took the house and the cow.' 'How do you mean? Were you homeless? What did you do?' 'My mum Olena found a job eventually, in a milk-processing plant. We were hungry.' Vera then makes a motion of her right hand scraping over her left. 'They made condensed milk at the factory. Mama scraped the machine clean at the end of each shift. She gave us this to eat. It was dirty-looking, thick sludge.' 'But what do you mean... Was it like some kind of a sweet... treat?' 'No, it was our food, our nutrients.' And then, without making any noise, her face crumpled and she took a breath that was meant to be deep but quickly turned into a cough. The few times she told me this story, there was always the hand-scraping action, quiet tears and the emotional-concealment cough. This memory of sticky sludge must have stuck for her, as it did for me. How can sugary gunk scraped off a machine be considered food? Why was condensed milk, a luxury, made at all, when the people cleaning the machines producing it were starving? I searched and found that a large milk-processing plant in Tyumen oblast was built right about the time of Vera's story. Did the milk come from the cows that were requisitioned from a family like hers?

I think of a painting by the Ukrainian artist Okhrim Kravchenko, called *Robbers*. In it, we see a gloomy man in a grey suit and a cap, holding an officious-looking book or a thick diary, and a whip. There is a blonde woman with a blue hat pointing with her hand outwards.

She too looks severe and officious. Another woman and a child clinging to her leg are wearing Ukrainian peasant clothing. The peasant woman is clinging to an emaciated-looking cow. All three — cow, woman and child — have their eyes closed and they look icon-like. The cow is being pulled away by a sheepish, angular young officer. The colours of the painting are dirty and dull and there are almost no shadows, which makes the whole thing look flat. There is such a strong feeling of dissonance, of helplessness in this painting, it pulls you in and spits you out again. And this is how I feel about all those people, including both my great-grandmothers, whose cows were stolen under the premise of some kind of 'policy'.

The milk-processing plant produced 1.2 million cans of milk in its first year alone. The plant's webpage boasts that a can was taken by Soviet astronauts into space in the 1970s and that an astronaut gazed down at Tyumen oblast and said that the region looked like a big heart at the centre of Russia. Vera, who would never have looked at her life from above, felt like she was living in the heart of darkness.

I kept pushing her. Things must have improved with time? You must have eaten normal food? I just couldn't fully comprehend the deprivation. She finally conceded and cheered up. There was a story she enjoyed telling. Her mother made simple flour-and-water flatbreads, Russian lepyoshki, the equivalent of Ukrainian korzhyky. Vera used to nibble around hers, carefully, so you could not spot the toothmarks. She would then put it over her younger sister Klavdiya's flatbread and say, 'My flatbread is smaller than yours! It's unfair, let me fix that!' Then she bit around her sister's flatbread like a rodent, to 'make them even'.

'What about pelmeni, babushka? Which meat did you use?' Vera's eyes widened. 'What meat? We had no meat, dorohenka moya ("my darling"). We filled them with potatoes.' The pelmeni of Vera's youth were stored in great big sacks left standing outside the house, a natural freezer, as temperatures outside hit -20°C.

Going to school every day in the winter was not an option. They only had one pair of winter shoes between the three sisters, a sad irony, given that her father had been a cobbler. 'I loved mathematics, and I loved school. I wanted to study, but I didn't get to finish more than four years.' The inner edges of her eyebrow muscles twitch up and in. 'Once I nearly died. It was too far away from home, in that weather. The winters were hard, the winds were so strong that there were ropes going from one house to another; we held on to them tightly with both hands, so the wind did not blow us off our feet.' But one day she grew tired. It felt like she was in the eye of a blizzard. She did not know where to go or how to keep on walking, so she lay down in the snow. The circular sound of the snow all around her made her feel calmer, lulling her to sleep. She said she was lucky that someone passed by. They picked her up and put her in a cart. 'Babushka, and you still wanted to go to school! Even after that!' My mother flashes me a look: give her a break. Vera stares forwards, as though into the snowy whiteout of her past. She says that she often stayed at her teacher's house, who was kind to her and gave her food and warm clothing, and once, a book. She cried telling that story, too; the memory of feeling so vulnerable, but people being kind, will do that to you.

There is a big gap in Vera's story. For however often she mentioned her fear of war, she didn't directly experience it. She remained around Maslyanskaya throughout her teens. Her daughter, my Aunt Valia, says that the only thing she knows is that Vera worked from the age of fourteen in a shop. So, in 1942, she was working her first job at a small shop near to where she grew up. She never did finish school, but her maths was good, and they needed people who could make calculations.

And then she got married. Vera did not like talking about her first husband, Ivan. 'What did you like about him, babushka?' 'He played the accordion!' 'Oh… he was fun? Were there fun times?' 'Yes. But he drank too. Too much. Oooooh, too much.' Their daughter was born, they called her Valia after Vera's older sister. They had a daughter, there was an accordion, but there was also drinking.

In *City of Bread*, an autobiographical novella by Alexander Neverov, published in 1923, Neverov describes the end of the Russian civil war and the movement of people fleeing the war-devastated and starving areas around the River Volga to Uzbekistan, where it was rumoured the bread was cheap and plentiful. I read the book a few years ago, hungry for descriptions of what Uzbekistan may have looked like and smelled like two decades before Vera ended up there.

Graphic descriptions of lice as big as ants crawling in a man's beard, a young woman suffering from dysentery emptying her bowels in front of everyone on a train, newborns gnawing on exhausted milk-less breasts, people squabbling, people dying. Most of the novella consists of descriptions of shit, blood and lice and there is just one word of dialogue during the long 3,000-mile (4,800-kilometre) train journey the hero embarks upon. Towards the very end, there is a short description of Tashkent. We feel the hot, stifling air of a semi-desert climate. I will translate a passage: 'Along the paths in the Tashkent gardens, mysterious, outlandish carts with huge wheels. Well-fed horses with ribbons in their manes and tails rattled their bells. On top of the horses sat strange, unusual-looking men, their heads tied, and thick white dust rose from the wheels, obscuring the trees and gardens, making it impossible to see anything.'

The mass movement of people to Tashkent continued for years. During the Second World War, when the Germans invaded the USSR, millions of people were encouraged to evacuate from the western parts of the Soviet Union to its faraway Eastern Republics.

THE NIGHT BEAUTY

In 1943, hundreds of thousands of Crimean Tatars and koryo-saram (Soviet Koreans), as well as citizens of other nations whose areas had been occupied by the Nazis, were accused of collaboration by Stalin and forcibly deported to remote parts of Central Asia, including Tashkent. Vera, Ivan and Valia went there in the 1950s. To Russians, it was a desirable destination, as the climate was hot and the bread was still cheap.

My Aunt Valia, who was six when she first went there, does not remember much, just the arid, lung-burning heat and huge watermelons and elongated yellow melons dragged on donkey-drawn carts along the streets, leaving a veil of stifling, sweet aroma and dust. But judging by the photographs, Vera loved it. There are a few pictures of her surrounded by primordial-looking plants, possibly canna lilies, most probably taken in the botanical gardens. There is one I love the most, another high-contrast black-and-white photo. Who took it? Who had the camera at that time? Vera is next to a friend with an expression of gaiety, albeit of a perplexed kind. Vera looks blissfully in-the-moment happy. She and her friend, side by side, young fresh faces, bemused. You can imagine them both thinking, 'How did we even get here? Were we inserted here by some kind of a trickster deity, because it feels unreal, it is way too much fun, and it is way too beautiful and wild.'

Tashkent was an ancient city-state of the Silk Road. It had been captured by Russian forces in 1865 who built a new city next to the existing capital. By the time of the Bolsheviks, Tashkent was two cities: the old town for the locals; the new town for Russians. It was inevitable that one would eventually swallow the other. But, for now, the Tashkent of the 1950s was green. There was an extensive process of 'greenification' of Central Asia during the years of the Russian Empire. Huge trees were casting a shade throughout the flat, hot city. A collage of Vera's new life there would include ikaat clothing, a strange mix of Islamic and monumentalist Soviet architecture, newly built apartment blocks, metallic shiny scarfs from bazaar vendors, a lot of purple, fountains, wide streets, busy markets, blazing sun and boat hats made out of newspapers, googly-eyed cars and trams trams trams. By the time Vera and Ivan arrived, the traditional makhalla low-rise communities had been bulldozed off and Soviet apartment blocks put up in their place. Because there was this constant influx of people from the European parts of the USSR, the Soviets urbanised Tashkent and made it sprawl.

Ivan, according to Aunt Valia, was a skilled worker. He found a job as a slesar, a word which mysteriously translates to 'locksmith' in English dictionaries, but which actually means 'technician at a factory'. Perhaps because of his job, they were assigned a two-bedroom apartment with high ceilings. There was an unusually large bathroom and a big kitchen. There was a courtyard with outsized fig trees, trees that neither of them had ever seen before. But the most remarkable feature was the gazebo, entangled with a vine that defied little

Valia's imagination. The vine was a beast of its own, an organism, dangling and tumbling and literally groaning over the gazebo table and benches. The grapes were as thin and long as her index finger and the bunches were huge, almost cumbersome, weighing two kilograms each at least.

Life couldn't be better after the desolation of a Siberian train stop, right? But Ivan started drinking even more. According to Vera, but denied by Valia, he got into a drunken brawl and killed a man. 'Babushka, how did he do it? Do you know?' 'He was an alcoholic. He hit someone's head with a bottle. He was imprisoned. And I divorced him.' Subject closed.

The large apartment they lived in was divided up, turned into a komunalka, a communal living apartment. Another two families were moved in. Vera and Valia moved into the kitchen with a stove by the north-facing wall; they propped a bed by the window. The bathroom was split into a smaller bathroom and a communal kitchenette, with a small table and a two-ring stove. The other two bedrooms were taken by the new families.

Vera's plan after her divorce was to further her limited education. She wanted to take a luggage cashier course in Samarkand, in order to then be assigned a job at the Tashkent train station. She took Valia back to Siberia and left her with her mother Olena.

Life was a motion blur in those couple of years. Siberia to Uzbekistan and back, to and fro and to and fro, trying to manage a new life as a working mother on her own. Then one day, on the way back to Tyumen to collect Valia for the umpteenth time, Vera was approached by a young man from Ukraine. He was wearing a green military uniform, which complemented his hazel-green, slightly crooked right eye. The absence of the other was the result of shrapnel wedged into his head, as she discovered later. He exuded confidence, had a full head of chestnut hair, large hands and a beautiful baritone voice. It was 1955.

When I was little, the story that was most often used to illustrate my grandfather's charisma involved him entering a field and stumbling upon an accordion. He picks it up and teaches himself to play it. Just like that. I imagined him mythical. I saw a huge, muscular back wading through a sea of golden wheat, playing a song about Moscow's tears on a green piano accordion with burgundy bellows. Nothing was beyond his reach.

Vera rushed through the story of their meeting, telling me he lured her in with an exotic English card game and his accordion-playing skills. But my imagination was never too far behind, and I can conjure the scene of their meeting from their faded photographs, as well as from train scenes garnered from life, books and movies. Vera's lips – red earth in a bow – cheekbones high, hair half-up half-down in dark brown fluffy finger waves, eyes small but expressive like toasted almond flakes, dark arrow-like eyebrows and a nose that looked like a young potato. She was already in conversation with someone sitting to her right, it always took her only a few minutes to make a new friend wherever she went. But the passenger opposite, who had hangover breath and three-day stubble, whipped out a bottle of vodka and a jar of brined pickles and started bashing a boiled egg on the edge of his seat. Will the ladies join him?

Suddenly, a saviour strolls up the carriage.

'Madmazel, would you like to play a card game with me and my comrades?' 'I like card games, which one are you playing?' 'It is called King!'

He uses the English word 'king' and it sounds impressive.

'Do you play an instrument?' 'Of course, the bayan [accordion]. I taught myself.' 'All right, I will play the game.' 'There is just one rule... You have to provide your name and address on this piece of paper.' 'What kind of a rule is this?'

Lyonya was too young to have fought in the Second World War, so he must have joined the army in the early 1950s. When he met Vera on the train, he was coming back from Chukotka, an area in far north-eastern Siberia, a mere 40 kilometres along the Bering Strait from Alaska. Lyonya told Vera that he was testing weapons, and that the wound in his head and the eye that he lost were both from these military test exercises. We now know that wasn't the case; in fact, the Soviets were testing nuclear bombs in the wilderness of Chukotka, a land inhabited by deer and indigenous communities.

They parted ways at Moscow's train station.

The letters from Lyonya started coming almost immediately. Vera talked about them until her death, if not with warmth, definitely in disbelief. 'Oooooh how he wrote! Krrrrasiiiiiivo. Beautifully.' She elongated vowels and rolled her 'r's strongly. 'No one ever wrote to me, ever spoke to me using such beautiful words.'

When I look through Vera's old photos, I can see some evidence of his tender eloquence. He had a habit of writing small vignettes on the backs of photographs, like snippets from a diary. In one of the pictures, Vera is in Tashkent. The photograph is high-contrast black-and-white. Vera is standing on a bridge flooded with winter sunshine. She looks elegant in a coat and hat and high-heeled ankle boots. She is leaning against the balustrade and it looks like she is staring into the distance, but on the back, Lyonya has written in Russian, 'Here is my Verochka on a bridge, looking at me, thinking how wonderful it is that I arrived.' In another photo, more dazzling light from the Tashkent sun. This time it is pouring over Vera's left side through a lace-curtained window. Her head is down, lips forming the crescent of a beatific smile. She is writing a letter with a quill pen. On the back, Lyonya writes, 'Verochka is writing a letter. I am not disturbing her, because I understand that letters should be written in a calm atmosphere.' In yet another, they are in Voznesensk, in the driveway my book photographer Kris and I will roll into in 2014. My four-year-old dad is a fast-moving blur. Lyonya's face is close to Vera's, nuzzling her cheek, the good eye in view, peeping at the camera. But there are warning signs: his hand is placed firmly on the back of her neck.

Vera wrote back. Nine months later, Lyonya arrived in Tashkent.

They married in winter and there was no wedding; they had no family there and no roots in Uzbekistan. The local weddings were three-day-long feasts, the bonnets of wedding cars covered with strips of green-and-red velvet and adorned with flowers, but Vera and Lyonya simply went to the registry office. Vera didn't even take off her coat or the goat's-wool scarf wrapped around her head and cheeks. I still have the photograph, or at least one half of it; the part with Lyonya in it will be ripped off in the 1960s. It wasn't a quick rip, a plaster-off kind of rip. It was careful and deliberate. She did not want to accidentally rip any part of herself from the photograph, but she wanted him gone.

At some point, they went back to Ukraine and collected Lyonya's mother Anastasiia to come and live with them in Tashkent. Anastasiia was a tiny woman, *interesnaya*, as Vera used to say: interesting, unconventionally beautiful. Incidentally, like my mum's side of the family, she also had Moldovan-Ukrainian roots. Their first year together was idyllic. From the photos, I can deduce that there was passion, pretty words, fragrant plov and sunshine. And then my father came along. Soon enough, Lyonya started complaining that the heat of the previous summer was shooting pain straight through his head wound, like a fresh piece of shrapnel. He couldn't spend another summer in Tashkent. He started drinking, they started fighting. When Dad was just three months old, Lyonya insisted they move to his native Ukraine.

I am not sure why they didn't go back to Vynnitsya oblast, where Lyonya was from. Years later, my dad received a phone call from someone claiming to be his half-brother. It is possible that Lyonya had a family there, as in a wife-and-children kind of family. Instead, Lyonya asked around for suggestions of a good place to live, and someone recommended the city of Mykolayiv. It was a port city, in Southern Ukraine, so it would be warm, but not so warm that it would affect Lyonya's injury. They arrived with a crate containing their possessions, but it was impossible for them to settle there. It turned out that they could not get a propiska, a residency permit. So someone else recommended a smaller town called Voznesensk. It was nice too, they said, there was a small river running through it and Anastasiia would feel at home, as every house was painted a distinctive blue that was common all over Moldova.

I have more gaps in the story, so I phone my Aunt Valia. 'First they built a Finski domik,' a Finnish house, a prefabricated wooden house. 'Dad's head wound gave him official status as an invalid, so he received benefits and was given a plot of land on the Bolgarka edge of Voznesensk.' While they all crammed into the Finnish box, they started building the main house. The summer kitchen was first. Valia remembers helping to make the traditional clay bricks called lampach. All through the summer, she and Anastasiia mixed clay with water and straw and worked it with their feet like a barrel of grapes. 'She would tie her platok [scarf] under her chin. We stomped and we sang, Olia. It was magical. Babushka Nastia had a beautiful voice, she was tiny like a nightingale and she sang like a nightingale.' 'What songs did you sing?' 'They were old songs. Ukrainian songs, and songs in Moldovan [Romanian] too. Those I couldn't follow at all, so I just listened.'

The extent of the fire in Lyonya's character revealed itself just after my dad's first baptism. The way the story is told is always the same. And however hard I press for details, they are not there. Yet I try again. I ring my dad. 'Pa, do you have five minutes?' 'Yes, yes.' 'Tell me again the story of your baptism.' His face crinkles and his white beard fills the screen. A hearty 'Ahahahahahahaha!' He loves this story.

'So they take me to the church…' 'Wait, were you allowed to baptise people, I thought you weren't allowed in the 1950s?' 'Yes, yes, we were allowed.' 'Wait, how old were you?' 'Well, small, a few months old, you know how early these things happen. So they go to a church and they baptise me. I piss on the priest, standard. And then Father has this massive row with my godfather.' 'Wait, what was it about? Do you know?' 'Ooooolechka! He could have a fight about anything at any time. You know what he was like. He probably disagreed about something, and then started shouting, swearing like a sailor, and went red in the face. So listen.' I'd heard this story a million times, but he is so excited. 'And theeeeen, the next day, he asks another couple to come and baptise me! So I was baptised twice!' I know that he thinks this is a sign of good luck, despite the shouting and the swearing that time and many more times. I'd heard people bring this up over and over when making toasts to Dad on his birthday: my father was baptised twice, that's why everything went so well for him in life.

Lyonya's surname (and my original surname) was Hrebeniuk, from hreben, 'comb' in Ukrainian. In Lyonya's case, a cockerel's comb. Vera said that he had brothers, and the Hrebeniuk brothers had a reputation in their native village. They loved a fight.

Vera got a job as an administrator at a local grocery store. Lyonya, who was on benefits, also secured an illegal side-job as a freelance mason. He was very good with his hands, and built houses for people.

It is worth mentioning that not all invalids were treated like Lyonya. I wonder if his injury, inflicted during secret nuclear testing rather than the war, put him in a different, more elevated, position. During the Second World War, General Zhukov used the infamous 'human wave attacks' to de-mine the fields leading to Berlin. 'Do not spare any soldiers! The broads will birth some more!' The official statistics say that 8.7 million Soviet soldiers were killed. Millions more were wounded, including hundreds of thousands who suffered life-changing injuries, including lost limbs. Thousands of mutilated soldiers returned to the USSR after the war, strewing the streets of Soviet cities and towns. The dissident Russian writer Liudmila Ulitskaya writes about seeing invalids on the streets of Moscow: 'There were thousands of them. No, millions, and it wasn't an exaggeration, but an understatement.'

Those who could live independently were given benefits by the state. Those who could not often chose not to go back to their families, so as not to be a burden. Accused of parasitism and political unreliability, many turned to drink. Double leg amputees, covered in medals, blind drunk on a 'scooter', a makeshift skateboard for moving around without legs. They were given cruel nicknames, reportedly invented by medical workers, which caught on. Double amputees were called samovar, after the tubby Russian teapot which was commonly animated in children's books as a face with a nose, but no arms or legs. Burn victims were called Quasimodos. Lyonya would have been a 'flounder', a flat fish, as one of his eyes was damaged.

The homeless invalids were regularly picked off the streets and transported to distant ex-monasteries, invalid sanatoriums, badly funded, to get them away from the Soviet victory myth. The authorities were only interested in the scrubbed-clean narratives of heroism and victimhood; grassroots memories that didn't adhere to the mythology were thus also scrubbed and altered.

Anastasiia was holding their family unit together. Lyonya would rage and she would diffuse. She also looked after the children.

Dad again. 'She read to me, Olia. She read books to me. It was unusual. I loved her so much. And then she was gone. I was five, I think, and I was there when she collapsed. She went to get some water from the well. She came back carrying a thing, you know what a yoke is? She was carrying a heavy yoke with two buckets, and then she groaned, put them down and just fell.' Anastasiia had suffered a stroke and spent about a year bedbound. It was a slow, year-long journey to death. Vera nursed her gently until the end. She got on with Anastasiia so well that she reserved a place at the graveyard right next to her. She wanted to be buried alongside her. Life with Anastasiia was so comforting, she wanted that comfort to carry on into the realm of beyond. I have been to that grave. Shiny granite headstones with their photos. Three in a row. Anastasiia and Vera right next to each other. Then Vera's third (beloved) husband.

After Anastasiia's death, an opportunity came up and Lyonya grabbed it with his two spade hands. He took a job as head of security at a sausage factory, an enviable position. Being head of security meant that theft was easy, so the loft in their house was always full of air-dried sausages: a true luxury. 'Olechka, I would just climb up to the loft, and literally there were dried sausages swinging at you like boxing bags. I wouldn't even look, just pull one down and gnaw at it, like it was a carrot.'

Lyonya's operations at the sausage factory were shady. Being head of security didn't only enable small theft; he was involved in much bigger operations. He used to pack huge amounts of cured meat on to secret wagons and send them off to Russia, organised and paid for by Communist Party officials. The smaller personal thefts were not frowned on so much, as for many it was a way to survive (wages were incredibly low and so many people struggled to feed their families). But Lyonya's full-scale sausage-heist operations reflected perfectly the rotten system, where just a few per cent of Communist Party elite were living a life of luxury while the rest of the population lived hand to mouth.

Vera's older sister Klavdiya arrived from Siberia to help once Anastasiia was gone, but Klavdiya saw through Lyonya and called him out in the most dramatic ways. And Lyonya's behaviour at home became more erratic and violent by the day. Dad remembers these years in the same way that he tells me about his baptism. I always found it hard to grasp: a story of violence told with hilarity.

Consider these two stories.

The first is the tragic side of the coin. One day, Vera came home in a beautiful new coat. It was made from an exciting new material called Bologna. It was an ankle-length, quilted, rainproof coat, a prototype of the puffer jackets we wear today. She had saved for it, she swindled its procurement and she sparkled in it, with the sharp bow of her brick-red lipstick perfectly complementing the quilted chocolate-coloured squares. Lyonya was not impressed. First of all, she had not consulted him about this extravagant purchase. Secondly, she looked way too good in it. In a jealous rage, he ripped that coat in two while Vera was still wearing it. This story is told with furrowed brows, by Vera, Aunt Valia and Dad.

The other story, told by my dad, was from the years while Klavdiya was staying with them. Both Dad and Aunt Valia adored Klavdiya. She was wiry, with dark hair and deep-set eyes shaped like two fish swimming towards each other. She had one dimple on her left cheek. Dad employs all his comedic actorly talents to tell this story, gesticulating wildly. After another early-morning row, he witnessed slender, sharp-edged Klavdiya — wearing only her nightie and armed with a broken Primus gas lantern — chase square-backed Lyonya, wearing just his baggy, striped briefs, out of the house and all the way down the street. Lyonya leaps towards the neighbour's rickety fence, Klavdiya hurls the Primus at him with an axe-thrower's precision, Lyonya rips a plank out of the neighbour's fence and catches the sharp nose of the lantern on the end of the plank. 'It was like a Bollywood movie, Olia.'

Lyonya, however, was not the only drinker. Klavdiya drank too, but quietly, in the evenings with a friend, hitting the bottle to soothe the outcomes of stories that were unspoken. And it was painful. My Aunt Valia acknowledges the drinking, but she is quick to add that her aunt was always well-turned-out, with sharp suits and make-up, a neat hairdo and little imps dancing in her eyes. She was feisty and vain, so when passports were given out for the first time in the 1970s, she changed her birth year to 1932, making her four years younger.

Vera often said, 'Why did you do this? You have just added four years to your working life, you will get your pension four years later!' Unfortunately, Klavdiya did not live to get her pension. Her drinking became harder and more lonesome. She died of alcohol poisoning in her early fifties. Her daughter and grandson suffered a similar fate. Both became alcoholics, and first her daughter, then son disappeared one day. Presumed dead. By the time I was born, there was no one left who was connected to Vera's old life in Siberia.

Vera finally divorced Lyonya when Dad was nine years old and Aunt Valia was finishing school. Lyonya did bring alimenti (child support) to their house, but Dad just threw it back at him over the fence. Mum always describes their characters as 'a match': so quick to anger. We were not to talk about Lyonya, or rather we were not to compare his character to Dad's. If we ever did, a match ignited immediately.

Vera, who became a twice-divorced single mother at forty, didn't stop living. She liked to go on trips to faraway places. There are photographs of her next to a stone eagle in Pyatigorsk in the Northern Caucasus, snow-capped mountain peaks looming in the background. There is another next to the Greek-style columns of the mud baths building in Yessentuki. There is a spring-time picture from Kislovodsk, another spa town. She was very free. One of the letters from my twenty-year-old mum to my dad reveals, 'I went to see Mama Vera, she had a gentleman over. She said it was strictly "for business". They drank all your coffee, Petya. Only five sachets left.'

Vera was already in her early sixties when a neighbour told her about a widower called Andriyovych. They met and started living together very soon after. It was a partnership that felt deep and eternal, another grave Vera wanted by the side of hers. Andriyovych was about ten years older than Vera, but he was still sprightly, his mind so sharp I always pictured it filled with chisels. They rose at 5 a.m. and dug potatoes together, cooked and cleaned, played cards to relax. They lived happily until Andriyovych died from ripe old age, in his early nineties. Like Liusia after Viktor's death, Vera started falling apart, stopped gardening and eventually could not get out of bed.

I was in Ukraine with my new husband-to-be Joe and took him to meet her: 'Look, Grandma, this is the one.' I remember she had very dry lips on that visit and I put some of my ointment on them, some Blistex, which calmed her. She kept saying spasibo – 'thank you' – so I left it behind for her.

Vera's death was very different to Liusia's. She stared death in the face for a good three months. She was bedbound and scared, panicking and hallucinating. That must have been tough and I did not realise just how bad she was feeling. It was as though all her life's demons were in the room and they were clawing at her face and chest; everything that she had missed out from her story to me was revealing itself in terrifying monstrous visions. She died soon after.

Olga at an assembly, School No: 2, Voznesensk, 1975

5

The Language of the Nightingales

It is 7:30 in the evening at the end of summer 2022 and I am sitting in my garden in London. I have neglected the garden over the recent growing season and left it to self-seed, so it looks unruly and wild, with flowering grasses, docks and chickweed tangled with winding nasturtiums, mint and sorrel. My eyes are darting between the different shades of green, from the sun-faded lime of the marjoram plant to the orange-green of the peach tree, which looks stressed.

I am sitting in my fold-out chair and sending voice notes to my cousin Ira, Aunt Zhenia's daughter and Ihor's sister. (It was Ihor whose house in Italy my parents escaped to in April 2022.) Ira has been with Mum and Dad in Italy this afternoon. They have decided that it would be best for them to stay in Berlin, near Ira and Ihor, while they wait for Kakhovka to be de-occupied, and therefore Ira was helping them with their German refugee support application. We send voice messages to each other because it is much easier than phone calls; we can dip in and out while we cook, or attend to children, or garden or work.

I have been trying to piece together the story of my great-grandparents Moisei and Yaryna, of my grandmother Liusia, their daughter, and wondering about Lenin's policy of Ukrainizatsiya. I wonder if Liusia was able to study in the Ukrainian language in the late 1920s when she went to school, or if her teachers taught in Russian. She and my grandfather Viktor spoke Ukrainian at home and I now regret that I never asked her about this before she died. I also wish I had asked her about her childhood home, Moisei and Yaryna's house and farm in Rakove. Did they feel as though that house was the final destination, a place to plant roots, or was 'home' a washed-out uncertain sort of notion, as it is now for my parents?

Today, though, I have a very specific question for my cousin. 'Ira, tell me again the Lenin story. I remember that we were at Aunt Liuda's that day, was it 1987?' The Lenin story was a top-ten story in our family repertoire, circulated and chewed over alongside the food pretty much every time we got together. I can picture the room, but the conversation, even if I did remember it, I was too young to understand. I was three years old then and Ira was fifteen. 'Take me back there,' I ask Ira. 'Give me sounds, smells, feelings!' I want to try and remember it all.

'Olechka, we were at Aunt Liuda's. It was a celebration of some kind... possibly her birthday. It was autumn, real autumn, it was getting cold and the trees were yellow and brown. Inside, in the living room, the table was extended and covered with a cloth and Liuda had already laid out the dishes when we arrived. The house, as you know, was low-ceilinged and cave-like, very cosy, whitewashed but dark. We were all sitting at the table and, as always, she had made lots of holubtsi [stuffed cabbage rolls] and also stuffed peppers. It was a given that she'd made a cake, either smetannyk or Day and Night cake, you know the ones, layered with sweetened vanilla crème fraiche. Mmm, what else? Well, you know Aunt Liuda really could cook. And I remember that I was in such a cool mood.'

Ira uses the word prykolniy, 'cool', and the way she says it contains a lot of information. How a teenager can feel cool when she hangs out with adults, almost like an equal. At last, a step closer to adulthood, she felt confident to join in their conversations.

'I can't remember why we started talking about Lenin. I think I asked a question about him.' Her deep, raspy voice rises up. 'Ahhhh, yes, I remember! I was already quite a big girl, a proper teenager. It was perestroika, the time of new ways of thinking, and we were starting to "peel off the layers", so to speak. At first,

Stalin. Then Brezhnev... Lenin was the bottom layer, close to the bone. But we hadn't reached the Lenin layer quite yet.'

Her voice jumps up again. 'Ahhhh! I know, so I defended Lenin! Lenin had good intentions, I said. My position was actually the official position, which was still taught to us in school at the time. And everyone who was listening to me, my parents, the other adults... their responses were kind of evasive, very mild, along the lines of, "Well, yes, dochenka [little daughter], you could put it like that, yes..." And then Petya, your tato [father], did his signature eye popping. You know his eyes are actually quite small, but they really pop out at moments like this, when he feels passionate. So, eyes all out, he almost shouts... well he doesn't actually shout, but says very intensely, "Why are you doing this to this kid? Hanging noodles over her ears [lying]! Enough! Stop keeping up this rotten talk."'

Hniliye razhovory ('rotten talk'), in Dad's Russian with a Ukrainian accent, sounds expressive. I roll it around my mouth: hniliye. I feel like I can taste the party line. Putrid, like a pickle gone bad.

Ira continues, in the agitated voice of my dad, booming with emotion, 'Ira, listen to Petya! If I don't tell you this now, if you do not hear me now, your whole life you will live in these lies and you will be poisoned by these fables. Lieeeeeneeeeen! That bald fool on a tank, that lame old goat with a beard...'

Ira's voice becomes quiet, conspiratorial. 'And this I will never forget, Olechka. When he talked with his bulging eyes, this made me feel so scared. That this Lenin, who I thought was the good guy, was in an instant reduced to a goat with a beard. It was funny,' she giggles. 'I actually saw Lenin morphing into a goat, with his goat beard sticking out. But I smelled fear on myself, I felt it in my blood, Olia. Adrenaline, or something else, inside my body... Petya voiced something, as my dad used to say, "I podooooomat nelza": that thing you cannot even think, let alone say out loud.' She stretches that 'ooooo' inside podumat, the word 'to think' in Russian, like a noise coming out of a baby trumpet. 'This kind of free thinking was unthinkable. So it was scary and it was Petya against them all.'

'Ira, the story always ended with you crying...' I say. 'Tak, ya vidrazu zaplakala, I suddenly burst into tears... Laughter and fear and that drunken feeling of freedom. You know, it makes me want to cry all over again.'

Now I remember the atmosphere, what a huge moment it was. Dad had said 'no' to the system and broken what was unthinkable to break: the habit of accepting lies and lying, even to yourself, for the sake of survival. The effects of movchanka, the Great Hush, were so much deeper than I imagined. There hadn't only been The Unsayable, there had also been The Unthinkable. Dad called everyone out. He shocked them and kickstarted the first tiny bit of mental rewiring. Ira sends me her last voice note of the evening and says, this time in Ukrainian, 'I podumaty mozhna!' ('Now we could think!')

Russification was in full swing in Ukraine when my parents were children in the 1960s and 1970s. This was a set of policies, both official and unofficial, that encouraged each of the fifteen Soviet republics – with close to 130 languages between them – to become a single homogenised Russified whole, with one history, one future and one language: Russian. Russian was the only 'proper' language. The Ukrainian, Belorussian and Central Asian languages, among many others, were called ne perspektivniye: languages with no prospect, the languages of no promise and no future. Mum explains that, if you wanted your child to get anywhere in life, to get into university, to get a good job, you had to speak Russian. Russian became the language of being able to survive, and the closer to the Russian borders that Ukrainians lived, the more fiercely Russification worked.

Cultural and linguistic suppression wasn't new for Ukraine. In fact, I always found it incredible how, without statehood, with liquid borders and aggressive neighbours, despite all that, a distinct Ukrainian language had developed and flourished at all. In the 337 years during which the territory of modern Ukraine has existed, under the colonial rule of its various neighbours, there have been numerous prohibitions on the Ukrainian language and its predecessor, Ruthenian. Publications in

Ukrainian and works of Ukrainian history were anathematised or burnt; schools that taught in the Ukrainian language were closed.

In the Soviet era, there was a crafty, sneaky way to make everyone speak Russian. It wasn't forbidden outright to speak your own language, but from 1933 (the official end of Ukrainisation), the number of Ukrainian schools which had flourished in the 1920s during Korenizatsiya – the temporary policy of boosting Ukrainian culture – started to diminish. Hundreds of Ukrainian-language teachers were either executed or sent to gulags. From the 1950s, parents could even choose to stop their children from learning Ukrainian at school; all that was required was a written request to the head teacher. In 1929, Ukrainian had been the first language in 80 per cent of schools; by 1961, that had dropped to 64.5 per cent.

When my parents were children, there was only one Ukrainian school out of ten in Voznesensk: school number 1. The Ukrainian school was the worst because teaching in the Ukrainian language was not a prestigious vocation; the quality of teaching was lower. Mum says that only children from families with no aspirations went to the Ukrainian school. Or at least that was its reputation. She would often overhear her mother Liusia say, 'Well, where else would they send her, surely not to nomer odyn [number 1]!'

There was no chance of passing university entrance exams if your education was not in Russian. So most parents wanted their children to attend either the Russian school number 10 or Russian school number 2, which turned out the biggest percentage of university goers. My parents both went to school number 2. When I ask Mum about her school years, one of the first things she says is that, if you spoke Ukrainian, you were called selyuchka or selyuk: 'villager' in Ukrainian. A Ukrainian word used by Ukrainians to insult Ukrainians who spoke Ukrainian. A meta insult.

Ukraine was already called 'the periphery' by Russians. There are two different etymological explanations of the word Ukraine. In Ukrainian, krayina means 'country', and u krayini means literally 'in the country'. In Russia, however, they say that the name comes from the Russian word okraina, which means 'outskirts', or 'the periphery'. So, according to Moscow, Ukrainians were on the edge of things, and their country was a borderland furthest away from knowledge, high culture and success.

At school number 2, you were not permitted to sit next to whoever you wanted. In the front few rows, you had the hardest-working, smartest pupils. The back of the class, where the most hopeless cases sat, was called Kamchatka, geographically the most remote part of the USSR, way off by Alaska. This was also where you went to sit as a punishment for talking in class or messing around, a classroom gulag of sorts. All the desks in the classrooms were meant for two pupils sitting next to each other. As a rule, a boy would be seated next to a girl. In year two, the teacher sat my dad next to my mum in the hope that diligent, studious Mum would have a positive effect on unruly, ants-in-his-pants Dad, who often ended up stranded in Kamchatka.

They were both eight and a half that September. It was 1966. Mum was serious and focused and had two dark ringlets on the side of each temple. Her uniform was spick and span and she carried her satchel straight-backed and with a sense of purpose. Dad was freckly and slightly potato-nosed, almost too lively, restless. There is a photo of them sitting in the second row by the window. Mum is not smiling, her back is rod-straight; her arms, according to school protocol, are at a right angle, the right forearm resting over the left. Dad's posture is more relaxed: his arms are also folded but higgledy-piggledy; he smiles from the left ear to the right and you can see the gaps where he has lost some of his front milk teeth. Mum's eyebrows are black, like her mother Liusia's. The photo is black and white, but I know that the wool uniform dress is maroon. Normally she would also be wearing a black apron, but here it is white with frilly straps – the apron for special occasions – and the occasion is 1 September, the first day of school.

Every 1 September was a real *prazdnik*, a 'festivity', a celebration. All the parents were there. Mothers in their best summer dresses, fathers with war decorations on show. The *raykom* secretary, a local Communist Party representative, would be there too. He would often make a speech, bookended by sharp-elbowed honorary salutes shouted out from the young pioneers. A loudspeaker would be used in the biggest schools, so people could hear all the way at the back. In between speeches, students would perform dances, usually ballroom style or, occasionally, an approximation of Ukrainian hopak (the Cossack dance... see? proof that we let you be Ukrainian). Special Soviet songs about schooldays would be blaring out, in Russian. 'On your chest, a red kerchief in bloom, like a river in springtime youth races through your veins. These are your school years, pioneer, and Komsomol [the Soviet youth group] awaits you!' At the end, a huge red flag with hammer and sickle would be laboriously hoisted above the crowd, who turned their heads up to watch it, faces beaming.

Soviet school interiors, just like Soviet apartments, looked pretty identical throughout the seventy years of the Soviet Union's existence. They all wore the same adornments. Without exception, Lenin's most famous testament, 'Uchitsa, uchitsa i uchitsa!' – 'study, study, and study!' – glowed white-on-red from school banners, reinforced with a picture of Lenin in profile, complete with his signature descending brow and small smile.

Political slogans and imagery were all around the school. Posters insisted that you owed it to your country to study otlichno ('to the highest standard'). The idea of 'owing' was everywhere. A typical poster from that era screamed, 'Let's work harder and return the coal debt to Mother Country!' A special 'Lenin room' was a necessary requirement in every school. In Mum and Dad's school, it was behind a stout, slatted wooden gate and contained a bust, more portraits, snippets of Lenin's early-years biography and more testaments, more slogans.

The first lesson of the first day of the week was always Politinformatziya, 'political information class', conducted by the head teacher. The teacher would open the newspapers: *Komsomol Pravda* or *Izvestia*, or, more rarely, the *Soviet Ukraine*. The first page was always about the achievements of the party, the following articles were about the roaring successes of the heavy industries and the working class. Then would come reports bashing the rotting Western empires and their long-suffering peoples. The Politinformatziya lesson was sometimes diluted with a little light reading: a short story or poem.

The bad news, the turbulent news within the USSR, did not exist on the pages of the newspapers, nor on the radio, nor on TV (which nobody had anyway, you were lucky to own a radio). Or if it did surface – a disastrous train crash, a catastrophic landslide, a nuclear accident – it was only reported with a great delay. Happy country, happy news.

'We were fifteen happy and free republics,' Mum says sarcastically. 'All together as the Soviet people. Tajik, Kyrgyz, Belarussian, doesn't matter, we are all building our lives towards the common aim: svetloye komunisticheskoye buduyusheye, "the bright Communist future". When I went up to my teacher and asked him, "When will this Communist future arrive?

Approximately, what year will this be? How long do we have to wait?" he did not give me an answer, because nobody knew, and because it was a lie.'

Mum learned the rules well at school and followed them. She was the perfect student. But Dad was different. We often joke that right from the start, from toddlerhood, he played by nobody's rules, not even his own. He was largely left to his own devices while his mother Vera went out to work. Even when his parents were still together, Vera had often taken shift work with unsociable hours. Dad was one of those kids who had their own house key on a ribbon, because there was often no one at home when he got back from school. He roamed the streets with older boys, swam in the river and messed around at the clay quarry.

He was clearly an odd one out, a joker, but also notably entrepreneurial. He collected rare stamps and sold or bartered them with fellow students. He was a dyvak, from dyvny – an adjective which can stand for both 'weird' and 'wonderful'. There was too much of an independent, individual spirit about him to fit into Communist society.

Once, when my parents were thirteen, their class was asked to write an essay about their favourite film. It was a duty to rank patriotic things as the best, so everyone wrote about Soviet war films. Mum wrote about *Liberation*, a two-part film about the Second World War. Dad, however, wrote about a French comedy called *Fantômas*. This was a James Bond spoof, but it was taken quite seriously by Soviet citizens, Dad included. Some Western films, especially French and Italian films, were allowed to be shown, as long as they complied with high moral standards and ideology and were deemed to be 'artistic'. *Fantômas*, with its car, train and helicopter chases, as well as its glimpses of French cities and countryside, was shown at the cinemas. Around 45 million Soviet citizens watched it: the movie was a craze. The walls of Mum and Dad's school were plastered in pieces of chequered paper that said 'Fantômas', the hero's calling card.

'*Fantômas* was our favourite too,' Mum says, 'but only Dad had the courage to write about it. The teacher said' (and here Mum puts on an astounded, thundering voice), '"Grebenyuk!!! YEDINITSA S MINUSOM!"' That means Dad's essay was marked as a one with a minus: a super-fail. Mum's voice becomes thin and mocking as she continues to imitate the teacher: '"My faaaaavooooourite film. What do you think he wrote about? *Fantômaaaaas*! As if there are no better films than this! He could have picked a film with a soul, a high-minded film!" And everybody burst out laughing. You know we roared with laughter, but not at Dad. More in a nervous way. We were outraged by Dad's bravery, the audacity of it! But he just shrugged his shoulders and replied, "You told me to write about my favourite film, so I wrote about my favourite film."'

The teacher loudly declared him a scoundrel and told him to get the hell out of her class. Being kicked out would have felt like the end of the world to Mum, but not to Dad. He strolled the school corridor undeterred.

Fantômas was still his favourite film. 'Kakoho chorta?' ('What the hell? I told the truth.')

Dad says his actions were not political, or at least, he did not recognise them as such at the time. He just did not understand why, if no harm came from it, he was not allowed to do something. He found it strange: the absence of bad news in the newspapers, or of good music on the radio. As a teenager in the early 1970s, he would stay up late to try and listen to forbidden radio, called the 'fake voices' in Soviet propaganda posters. To this day, people in Ukraine joke when I mention the BBC. They blurt out, 'Aaaaah Izhe si na BBC,' in reference to a 1970s poster, in which a slack-jawed Soviet citizen, on his knees, crosses himself before a levitating radio with a snake coiled around its receiver.

Soviet news, in common with the Politinformatziya lessons, drilled into listeners that the West was corrupt and failing and that everything in the Soviet Union was tickety-boo. But Radio Liberty, Voice of America, the BBC, German Waves and other Western radio stations broadcast their programmes in Russian, to counter the relentless Soviet propaganda in the USSR. The Soviets replied in kind. They too had a special radio station, Radio Moscow, broadcast in English and aimed at young socialists in Western societies. Dad did not know all this; he was just hungry for the music and also for a glimpse of something radical, of someone who might call Stalin a murderer, or Brezhnev an idiot.

There were huge Soviet radio signal-jamming stations planted in large cities, so living in a smaller town like Voznesensk was an advantage to Dad as he chased good music and a non-Soviet political narrative. The further you were from a jamming station, you see, the better your chance of catching 'the short waves'. During the day, Soviet authorities successfully jammed the enemy frequencies. But in the early hours, usually after 1 a.m., through the hissing static, you had a chance to hear from the West: a parallel dimension.

So while Vera was asleep and before the cockerel next door began shouting and it was time to go to school, Dad would sit with his ear against the radio, a Latvian VEF receiver, fiddling with the knobs. He wasn't always successful, often there would only be moments of clarity in a sea of wavering voltages and static scratch. But sometimes, sometimes, he would catch a whole twenty-second snippet of Led Zeppelin's 'Stairway to Heaven', Uriah Heep's 'July Morning' (his favourite song) or The Animals' 'House of the Rising Sun'.

When I ask Mum what she thinks about her school years, she says that most of her and Dad's childhood and youth were marked by the juxtaposition of the pompous and huge Soviet state and its actors against the feeling of being small. The idea of 'the people' was a blurry, intangible concept. All the achievements of the Soviet Union were quantified in terms of vague, grandiose numbers. 'The Soviet people produced X amount of steel this year.' 'The Soviet people have conquered the North Pole.' 'The Soviet people increased their military strength.' There was no bigger achievement than the Second World War, which everyone knew the Soviets had won almost single-handedly. (I thought that myself in the 1990s!) It is important to add that it has never been called the 'Second World War' in the USSR. Instead, it was known as the Great Patriotic War, implying both that it was the Soviet Union's war and that it was the Soviet people who had defeated the Nazis.

But one day, an Unthinkable happened. Mum and Dad's history teacher was replaced by a substitute teacher and she told them something unusual about the Great Patriotic War. She was the headmaster's wife and she had taken part in the Great Patriotic War herself. She had actually fought in it. Mum thought she was beautiful. Tall, small-waisted and curvaceous, like Sophia Loren, with a strict, dark-brown teacher's bun pinned at the nape of her neck.

Mum does not remember how it came about, but she will never forget the moment that the teacher, whose name was Averyanova, told them that the Great Patriotic War would not have been won had it not been for the American lend-lease scheme and the Allies. Facts that were missing from all the Soviet history books and from the hugely popular and numerous Great Patriotic War movies. Averyanova had seen it, she saw this help arrive with her very own eyes, in the form of food provisions, vehicles and weapons. She explained all this calmly, there was none of the usual exaltation, no heightened intonation. Mum describes her as ztrymana, 'composed': steady-voiced, her eyes piercing and cool.

That very day, Mum went home and asked her father if what Averyanova said was true. It was 6 p.m., Viktor had just got back home from his shift as a driver for a local kolkhoz veterinarian. Liusia had made borsch and there was a pile of korzhyky flatbreads on the table. He took a mouthful of the pink soup, swallowed, and in his usual soft and quiet voice, without moving his eyes from the plate, said in Ukrainian, 'Tak, tse pravda.' 'Yes, this is the truth.' And he carried on eating. He told Mum that one day he would tell her all about his Studebecker, but not now, he was too tired. And Mum knew, this conversation: it was over.

The system was supposed to work the same for everyone. You are born, you study; if you are lucky or have connections, you go to university, or else, if you are male, you go into the army; you enter the system of job distribution, or you go to work in a factory; you drink, you die. Liusia was extremely dismissive about those who lived happily within the system. 'Vodka, kovbasa i divan-lodka,' she would say, 'vodka, processed sausage and a sofa bed,' three things to carry you through life until you die from alcoholism and a rubbish diet.

It was her life's mission to get every single one of her six children into university, and not just to study anything. She wanted her children to be doctors, teachers or scientists. Her eldest daughter Zhenia became a primary school teacher. Valentina became a doctor, and that was Mum's aspiration too, as she excelled at chemistry. For the boys, if they did not go to university, they would have to serve in the army, which made university an even more attractive prospect. It was not easy to get into university, however, especially for degrees that were popular or had limited places. According to unwritten laws, young people with connections, or with enough money for a fat bribe, got through. The others, even if very bright, would often be deliberately failed. The exams were oral and it was easy enough for the examiners to ask a question that hadn't been covered in the official curriculum.

There was a sneaky selection process of cherry-picking top students from the small towns and villages for education in the military sector, which was the most important sector of the Soviet system. For example, Mum's eldest brother Viktor wanted to study physics at university. He was good at it and a science degree led to more prestigious jobs than a humanities degree. At his entry exam he was doing perfectly until, lo and behold, the last question proved impossible to answer. He did not get the place at the Odesa Mechnikov National University. Immediately after the exam, however, he received an invitation to take up a bursary in the Odesa Military Academy. There was even a common term for this – pokupateli – 'buyers', meaning that the military academies were 'buying' poor but bright youths by offering them free accommodation, plus the prestige of becoming a military man.

The most desirable university faculties were very competitive. Mechanical engineering had an average of four and a half students vying for each place. Medicine, even more. Dad's dream was mechanical engineering, with cars and tractors a speciality, but the electronics faculty had only a two-and-a-half person-per-place competition rate, so he applied for that instead. It was only after he passed, Dad says, that he realised that electronics had such a low competition rate because it was one of the hardest courses. He passed alongside physics and mathematics wunderkinds. He says, 'There were all of these prodigies, and me' (laughing heartily, thinking it must have been some kind of a fluke that he got in).

Despite Mum being awarded a golden medal at the end of her school career, she did not enter university until she was twenty. The first year, the authorities failed her in one of her exams (she had no connections or money for a bribe); the second year she had just given birth to Sasha; the third year she was missing six days of the required six months of work experience. (It had taken her sister Valya three attempts, three Augusts in a row, to pass the exam for medicine.) Mum was about to try for medicine again, but her family were all afraid she would be failed once more. Her dad Viktor talked to her; he said, 'Who wants to be looking at all those withered, sick bodies anyway, Olichka? Being a pharmacist is such a good profession, and you will be clean in your white coat.' She applied to study pharmacy, and this time she got in.

As a general rule, after university you entered the system of job distribution. In Russian they called it po rasspredeleniyu, 'according to distribution'. Heads of factories and other employers would visit universities and announce where they needed young specialists. Mum and Dad were not expected to go to a government-assigned place, however, because they had a small child, my brother Sasha. They were given a svobodniy diplom, a 'free diploma', and could choose to settle near family. So in 1983, they moved to Kakhovka, where Mum's sister Zhenia (a teacher) and her husband Sasha (a surgeon) had been distributed a decade earlier.

They found a tiny flat for rent in the same chip-walled Khrushchevka block as Zhenia and Sasha. I was born a year later. No one believes me, but I remember that flat in minute detail. It may have helped that every other flat in Kakhovka had the same configuration; in the USSR, the largest country in the world, most apartments were similar. Ours was cramped and shoddy. The walls were so thin that not even the Uzbeki rugs hanging on the wall could muffle the sound of the neighbours arguing or having sex. My parents slept in the living room on a fold-out bed. I was meant to sleep in a cot, but I cried and cried so they put me between them on their narrow mattress. Sasha slept in the tiny room we were not supposed to use, because that's where the flat's owners stored their things. But Sasha needed to sleep somewhere.

At first, Dad worked at what they called tele-atelier, as a TV technician. When Mum talks about this period, her voice is a mixture of tenderness and indignation. 'He used to fix TVs. He worked all the time, so much. And you know, those shitty Soviet lampovi televizory [tube TVs] broke all the time, so there was plenty of work, but there was no space to grow in that atelier.' And grow is something that Dad wanted to do. To experience change, movement, invention, adventure. He wanted to create something of his own... and he also wanted to get us out of the tiny apartment. I would get bigger soon, and I would need my own room. The kitchen was so small, it was difficult to do the usual things, the lengthy autumnal preparations, the jamming and fermenting. A summer kitchen was needed.

My dad has simple answers to my questions. When I ask him, 'Why did you hate the systema so much?' he answers, 'They forbade me to listen to the music that I loved.' Mum says he hated being patronised and he hated the feeling of being in a prison. The school was a prison, his job was a prison, there was nowhere to move forward. There wasn't an opportunity to grow and change, and it was growth and change that made life exciting.

One day, Dad came up to Mum in the morning, a cup of strong tea on the small Formica table in the tiny kitchen, Mum stirring pumpkin rice for breakfast, bright orange and smelling of sweetness, the rice starch, pumpkin and sugar. He said, 'Zaychyk [little hare], you wouldn't be embarrassed if I became a fireman, would you? I need time to figure out what to do, I want to build us a house.' So that you understand, to be a fireman in the Soviet Union was classed as an occupation for the idle. 'To sleep like a fireman' is an actual idiom. But Mum knew he was not lazy, so she said, 'Do what you need to do, if it will help our family.'

Firemen worked two shifts on, two shifts off, so during his two days off, Dad would have time to figure out how to supplement his income. He already had a plan to restore old Soviet Volga cars with a friend and sell them. And this is exactly what they did on his days off from sitting in a fire station (there were not a lot of fires in a small town like Kakhovka). He says he only went out once, when a pine forest caught fire, the result of a negligent forest picnic. He saved money from his tele-atelier gig to buy the first Volga and went halves with his friend. They did them up and drove them to Moscow, where they sold them in the market.

In one of my diaries, I find a transcribed conversation with Dad. 'The cars you used to restore in the 1980s, were a lot of other people doing this?' Dad, voice slightly indignant: 'No, what I did was pretty exclusive as I only restored Volgas, the most expensive car in the USSR at the time...' 'If I was to give an equivalent in Western terms, which car was comparable, Tato?' 'None, Volga was utter shit. Still, at the time, they were very expensive to buy new.' A new Volga cost 40K rubles, but a battered one was about 10K. 'And were you free to go, no one bothered you, asked you anything?' 'Yeah, it was fine, just the GAI [traffic police] always demanded something. Money or even lemonade.' 'What do you mean, lemonade?' 'They see you have three bottles of lemonade in the car and they say, "Give me one of those!" Sometimes we gave it, sometimes we didn't. Sometimes Mum would pack us an otbivnaya [a schnitzel], sometimes we stopped in cafés by the roadside.'

'Why did you stop doing it?' 'Why? Well, first of all, after a year or so it felt like Volgas were no longer as desirable, we were not making as much on those as we were in the beginning. But more importantly, I found a job at a fish kolkhoz. I was a supply engineer. One day, the director of the kolkhoz took me to Nikopol to a plant and showed me how they made things out of plastic there. I'd never seen how plastic was used before. Within three months, we had a workshop at the fish kolkhoz that was producing things made out of plastic.' 'Hold on, but this wasn't entirely legal?' 'We used plastic offcuts. Stuff that would have been put into landfill. They literally would have been burying these bits of plastic, so we got this plastic and we blitzed it into granules and repurposed it. And we didn't steal anything. We were allowed to keep 27 per cent of the profits, the rest had to go to the state. Still, at the time, all these heads of local Communist organisations, the municipal Communist heads, they were annoyed! So they gave instructions to the financial police to catch us out. But those OBKhSS guys [the Department Against Misappropriation of Socialist Property], they had very limited brain connectors, or none at all, so... they hid! Behind a derelict building and behind trees...' Dad's voice rises, this is a funny anecdote. The situation to him was ridiculous. 'They were trying to catch us loading or unloading some sort of illegal stuff, but there were just these plastic offcuts and they didn't really know what to do with that. But, eventually, they did shut us down. They said the fish kolkhoz is not the correct place in which to make things out of plastic.'

Dad's real break came as soon as the first cooperatives were made legal and some entrepreneurial activity began to be allowed. Too many people were already involved in private side hustles; too many to stop. And in 1987, when I was three years old, we moved from our crumbling Khruschevka in the centre of town to our new home on the suburban edge of Kakhovka. Dad had made enough money to build us the house he had dreamed of building.

Our new house looked like a home that a child would draw. A pointy roof, light brick, square-shaped. I had my own desk, and a single bed, and a fancy night light – a chunky, framed picture – that when you plugged it in, lit up into a blushed, half-opened rose. In the warm months, the elderly neighbour would bring his three goats to the green patch outside the fence, right opposite my bedroom windows, and they would bleat and wake me up too early for my liking.

But for me, the most important thing was that our house had two floors, a novelty and still a rarity in Kakhovka. The Soviet state had specific, limited house and apartment designs and two storeys was not permitted, at least not in Ukraine, as it was deemed too bourgeois. So I cannot stress how exciting it was, the wooden stairs going up into a stubby room which had a sofa bed and a cabinet filled with books, then two doors with milky, obscured glass, and the long narrow loft room, my brother's bedroom. The stairs felt symbolic, a means to climb up and out into a new life and into a different, exciting, if unknown, future.

Russification had been extremely successful, especially in the areas of Ukraine closest to the Russian borders, the east and the south. In the 1960s, even Aunt Zhenia opted her son Ihor out of learning Ukrainian at school. It was one thing that she regretted and, we suspect, wanted to make up for. In the 1980s, she became a member of the municipal education board and was a fierce campaigner for Ukrainian as the main language in Kakhovka's schools. She wanted to swap the system around, so that instead of just one school in town teaching in Ukrainian and the rest in Russian, it would be the reverse, with mostly Ukrainian-language schools and a single Russian school for those who wished to be educated in Russian. But even in the one Russian school, she wanted both Ukrainian language and Ukrainian literature to be taught as compulsory subjects. Did we not live in Ukraine? Would the French not teach their children in French or the Welsh in Welsh, these days at least?

Despite Zhenia's best efforts, however, none of us ever did switch to Ukrainian fully until the invasion of 2022. Russian language and culture were too deeply ingrained for so many, including me. It was our first language. With a simple Russian sentence – Idyot bychok kachayetsya, 'a little oxen walks and wobbles' – memories from childhood flood in, as this is a line from a Soviet book we all read as children. When I was growing up, a term of endearment within our family was kuzia, which was the name of a cute house spirit in a Soviet cartoon. It was incredibly difficult to stop using the language which encoded so much familial warmth. There were too many familiar, tender Russian words which were hard to let go, especially those that carried my Siberian paternal grandmother Vera in them, such as blinchiki ('pancakes') and babushka ('grandmother').

It is difficult to quantify how similar languages are, but I have seen research that states that Ukrainian is closest to Belarussian (80 per cent), Polish (69 per cent), Slovak (67 per cent), then Russian (64 per cent). The thing is, we Ukrainians understand Russians, but they don't understand us. From an early age, I understood Ukrainian fully but I wasn't able to speak it freely. Almost everyone in our region's towns spoke Russian. In smaller villages, a mixture of Ukrainian and Russian called surzhyk was often heard. We used it too, but mainly to joke around. To our ears, Ukrainian sounded warm but funny. Even when I was a teenager in the early 2000s, my dad used Ukrainian to make a joke. He started calling my boyfriend, who wanted to be a writer, the Ukrainian pysmennyk rather than the Russian pisatel, so every time he said the word, it stuck out. It was a regular Ukrainian word for 'writer', but it sounded as frivolous as 'scribbler'.

With the invasion of Crimea in 2014, families like mine paused and started thinking deeply about Ukrainian language and about Ukrainian literature. Why did I grow up believing Ukrainian literature was tedious and peripheral, but Russian literature was profound and globally important? Why did we use Ukrainian language in a pejorative way? Why did we use Ukrainian words to describe the silly or provincial? The word selo, 'village', which should evoke the most beautiful associations, was still used to call someone gormless and unsophisticated, even stupid. Just as it had been in Mum and Dad's schooldays.

Before 2014, all I heard through the Russified filter of my mind were the 'ugly' Ukrainian sounds, the guttural 'gh's that are so different from the hard Russian 'g's. Take my name, for example. In Russian, you say Olga with a hard 'g'. 'Ol'-gar'. In Ukrainian, it is softer, somewhere between an 'h' and a 'g'. 'Ol'-gha'. Now, I began to hear it differently. The Russian sound for 'g' is made with your tongue against the roof of your mouth. The Ukrainian comes from the chest. I can feel it where my heart is. Ukrainian vowels are extra melodic. The cadences are songlike. The phrase 'I love you', for example – Ya tib-ia liub-liu – is staccato in Russian. In Ukrainian it is legato: ya tebe kohayu. All those shh sounds and ye sounds and khh sounds: to me now, it is the language of the wild whispering grasses of the steppe, of the foaming waves of the Black Sea and the rustling tips of snow-dusted Carpathian silver firs. Solovyina, as we call it, 'the language of the nightingales'.

In 2014, when I started to try and speak Ukrainian, my thinking language was no longer Russian in any case. I had been living in England since 2003 and my thinking was firmly, routinely, organically English, even if my spoken English was not perfect. I even dreamt in English. So I thought: this can't be hard. But my attempts – and that of my family, and probably of the wider Ukrainian people, too – were clumsy. Russian words were wedged in hard, wired so tightly. They pushed their way out and sucked away our confidence. Mum and I settled on trying at least to message each other in Ukrainian. Much easier than speaking it, we thought, and good enough for now. One day we will learn to speak, one day.

Dear reader, I will tell you one way that helps speed up learning your native language: a genocidal invasion of your country. Suddenly, despite the shock and pain, or maybe in spite of it, we started to make an effort. It felt urgent to speak Ukrainian, and it felt good. It was an act of self-realisation, an act of self-preservation. An act of resistance. Russians say we do not exist? How can we not be, if here we are, alive and breathing and speaking our own language? With ease and pleasure to boot. There wasn't a magic trick to it, of course. It took time and it was difficult and awkward at first. It helped me to see a photo online, a sign in a café in Lviv, which read, 'Dear (displaced) Ukrainians. Please, do not feel shy making mistakes in Ukrainian. You are not funny. Vy chudovi. You are wonderful.' This was a kind and gentle message to all those who had fled to Lviv from eastern and southern Ukraine and feared that they would sound like idiots trying to speak Ukrainian in a broken, clumsy way. I embraced that message and felt freer. I started not to worry about the mistakes I was making.

The battle was not just to speak Ukrainian but to live it, to inhabit it. I was keen to educate myself. I had read all the Russian classics, the 'Tolstoyevskis', as a child, but I had not read one Ukrainian classical novel in my whole life. At school, Ukrainian literature had the reputation of being a drag. Not knowing the language well, it was harder to read and the themes were more difficult to grasp. So I decided to read *The Noblewoman* by the Ukrainian writer and activist Lesia Ukrainka. Ukrainka's mother was the famous Ukrainian writer and publisher, Olha Drahomanova-Kvitka (who went by the pen name Olena Pchilka, 'Olena the Bee'). Her father was a Ukrainian nobleman, Petro Kosach. Her real name was Larysa Kosach-Kvitka, but she chose to write under a pseudonym which literally means 'Lesia the Ukrainian Woman'. Lesia Ukrainka's play *Boyarynya, The Noblewoman* published in 1914, is set in the seventeenth century, following a truce between the Cossacks and the Russian Tsar.

The main protagonist is a young Cossack woman named Oksana, who marries a Ukrainian nobleman and moves with him from their native Poltava in central

Ukraine to Moscow. Oksana thinks it will be fine, the religion is the same and she understands a little of their language. But what she finds in Moscow is a total culture shock. She is not permitted to leave her house by herself and she is forced to cover her face when she is out. The women are kept separate from the men and are treated as subordinates. Whenever visitors come, the men and women do not mix. Confusingly, before retiring to the women's quarters, she is expected to kiss her husband's superior, who she'd just met that day, on his lips. A local custom, she is told. She misses home. This world is strange and limiting. She wants to go back, but she cannot. 'Her freedom crushed / Ukraine lies bleeding under Moscow's boot / Is that what you call peace? / A ruined wasteland.' I read it in one evening. I downed it thirstily, like a shot. It all felt so timely.

A few days later, I was in the kitchen chopping. I often say that if I could do nothing else except chop for the rest of my days, I would be happy. It's meditative, it's calming. Magical, wondrous things happen when you chop. I am mulling over the play. Oksana the noblewoman, the seventeenth-century dubious peace treaty... I think of Lesia Ukrainka. I know her birth and death dates roughly. I put down my knife and pick up my phone. I want to check Lenin's dates; I wonder if they were contemporaries. Russia has been saying that Lenin invented Ukraine, that it was Ukrainizatsiya in the 1920s that gave Ukraine its identity, which of course is absurd. How could there be Lesia the Ukrainian Woman if there was no Ukraine? 'Huh,' I think (in

English), surprised by what my phone tells me. 'Lenin was just nine months older. So how could he have invented her? She died in 1911!'

And then it happens. In my head, four round, simple and perfect words appear, with no effort or design or planning: Yak se mozhe buty? 'How can this be?' It is my first spontaneous thought in Ukrainian. A watershed moment, like Dad discovering the short waves for the first time, like Ira's vision of Lenin as a goat. A little thing that is a huge thing. The first five seconds of new pathways, new perceptions. The first five seconds of true freedom. I think, in English, 'I've come home. I'm in.' And then I try it out again, in a loud whisper. 'Ya Ukrayinka.' 'I'm Ukrainian.'

Zhenia, Kakhovka, 2005

6

A Lesson About Freedom

On day three of the war, 27 February 2022, my brother WhatsApps me a photo of himself. He is in his black-rimmed glasses as usual, black Nike joggers, a black jacket with a smidge of sunshine yellow around his left arm, black leather loafers, fingerless gloves, a white satchel on his left shoulder and a cap. He looks kind of normal, the Sasha I know, except perhaps slightly sportier and more serious in the face. The yellow band and the satchel are strange too. Also, astonishingly, there is a rifle. The rifle is hanging over his right shoulder and the body of the rifle is dark and almost invisible against Sasha's body, clad in black as it is. Only the barrel points down, thin, black and funereal. Sasha's right hand is hovering over it, not quite touching it, unsure. Later, he will send me a voice note, saying, 'Sonechko [little sunshine], it is not a satchel, but a bandolier, and it is not a rifle, it is a Kalashnikov.'

The text message below the photo reads, 'I decided to join the Kyiv Territorial Defence.'

My thoughts race and stumble over each other. Just the week before, Sasha had written to tell me that his new business, an eco-bike shopping delivery start-up, was going well. 'I signed a contract with SILPO' (a Ukrainian equivalent of Waitrose). He and his two sons had been whizzing around Kyiv delivering groceries. 'A whole bunch of electric scooters are on their way from China.' He had sent a photo of the three of them sipping flat whites in a café. Three similar smiles, a hanging basket of pink-and-grey-leaved 'string-of-hearts' against a foggy window, which means it is warm inside where they are, and cold outside. It is a scene from any European city, Paris or Madrid or London. How can it be that Sasha, who had previously never so much as touched a gun, is now holding a weapon?

I picture the city my brother lives in. The Kyiv where I used to stay each time I flew to Ukraine to visit. I think of the neat Airbnb I rented, right by the Golden Gate on the corner of Volodymyr Street and Yaroslaviv Val Street, the fortress gate of the ancient state of Kyivan Rus. The Golden Gate: the sacred entrance to Old Kyiv, parts of which have survived for a thousand years, a symbol of Kyiv's independence and defence, the ancient entrance for Byzantine envoys and Genoese and Armenian merchants. The gate to Europe.

I think of the Andriyivskyy Descent – my favourite part of town – in the summer, steep and hilly, cobblestones massaging the arc of my sandalled feet as I walk, stopping to photograph a weathered candy-pink door. The glow of the white-and-Swedish-blue of St Andrew's Church, the rococo frills of its façade and its plump malachite domes towering above us. The artists selling their painted canvases, souvenirs and textiles against the backdrop of massive murals, some depicting the murdered Ukrainian writers of the 1930s, the 'Executed Renaissance', some the Ukrainian activists killed during the Revolution of Dignity in February 2014. One of the best murals, created by Ukrainian and French graffiti artists, is 15 metres tall. It is called *Revival* and depicts a girl with a steady gaze and a flower wreath encased in a halo of sky-blue cosmic rays. Her long plait and colourful ribbons are traditional. She is holding a little boy in the palm of her right hand, while resting her left, gently and protectively, over a tumble of pretty houses: the city itself. Over her heart, an opening, a soul in the shape of a golden gate, with a blue-leafed tree of life standing proud in its entrance. The whole thing is huge and awe-inspiring, luminous, with at least ten shades of blue and accents of rusty red and paradise yellow.

In my mind's eye, I walk down the Kyiv streets to Podil, the hub of intelligentsia and young creatives, past Mohylyanska university students, the student-founded Khvyl'ovy bar speakeasy, the dilapidated gothic mansion on Verkhniy Val Street, the furniture shops, Stalinist apartment blocks. I think of the Yaroslava near St Sophia Cathedral, a hole-in-the-wall gem that sells tiny pyrizhky buns with all sorts of different fillings. A four-minute walk away from Yaroslava stands Kashtan coffee shop, serving various styles of coffee made by all sorts of extraction methods: some, such as Cascara infusions from the dried skins of coffee berries, are as delicate as tea. Cosy-small, draped by liana-like house plants, a record player and vinyls, oh, and a huge aviary, with pet ravens in the courtyard. Not even in London, my home, is coffee as hipster and cool.

I remember the Kosatka bar, where, one September, my husband Joe and I met a film-maker and his wife, long-skirted and white-haired like a mermaid, and drank too much Odesa Black wine. I think of the TCP bar on Lviv Square, its cocktails, its quirky tiled floors, Soviet-era cinema chairs and teacups, multi-coloured bar stools and beaded curtains. A restaurant called The Last Barricade which required a password to get in (Boritesya – Poborete, 'Fight and You Will Win', a phrase from Taras Shevchenko's famous poem 'Caucasus').

In spring, blooming panicles of chestnut trees, the symbol of Kyiv, drench the city's long main street with the warm scent of an old wool blanket and the colours of half-ripe strawberries and cream.

But now it is February, though the city is unusually dry and warm, Sasha tells me when I call him. There has been no rain and no snow. The morning frosts are sun-drenched and tender. Sasha slips from Ukrainian to Russian and back again when he speaks to me, but he consistently uses the Ukrainian word Lyutiy for 'February'. Lyutiy is also an adjective, meaning 'fierce' or 'furious'. Later, I look it up in the dictionary; it also means 'severe', 'wicked', even 'diabolical'. So yes, it was Lyutiy, but it was not fierce, or at least not until 24 February. Until then, February had been soft and spring-like. The world was twirling, spinning, hurling itself forward, like one of those Futurist posters from the 1920s, full of movement and speed. The last of the Covid restrictions had started to lift and the city was opening up. There was a feeling that the world was about to bloom, to unfurl itself like a leaf. 'It smelled of spring,' Sasha tells me. 'It smelled so much of spring.'

How was it possible that this city, this city bustling with youth, art and freedom, was under attack? It feels surreal, as if the dark murky past has seeped through some time-warp hole between dimensions like a monster and is trying to drag us back in, to undo the Ukrainian volya – which means both 'will' and 'freedom' – to steal our hard-won independence and smother the world of free-thinkers with its pock-marked tentacles of fear and lies.

It was in Poland in the 1980s that the first independent (anti-Soviet) trade union and workers' movement, called Solidarność, was founded by Lech Wałęsa. He was a Gdansk shipyard electrician who would be instrumental in getting Poland out of the USSR and who, in 1990, became the first democratically elected president of Poland since the 1940s. Solidarność, or Solidarity, doggedly pushed for freedom to protest and freedom of speech, for better healthcare, for workers' rights. It was a huge catalyst for the protest movements that mushroomed all over the Soviet Union, causing Soviet republics to chip off the bloc one by one, starting with Estonia in 1988, which asserted its sovereignty that very year (formally becoming independent on 20 August 1991). Revolts and demonstrations followed in the Caucasus, Belarus and Ukraine.

On 23 August 1989, 2 million people from Latvia, Estonia and Lithuania formed a giant human chain, later called the 'Baltic Way' or the 'Baltic Chain'. The USSR always insisted that the Baltic States had joined the Soviet Union of their own free will, but that was not true. There was a secret agreement between Nazi Germany and the USSR in 1939, called the Molotov–Ribbentrop pact. This pact essentially divided Eastern Europe between Nazi Germany and the USSR, with the Baltics falling under the USSR's direct influence. In 1941, more than 50,000 Baltic citizens were forcibly deported, in cattle trains, to northern parts of Russia, just as my grandmother Liusia had been in the 1930s.

On the fiftieth anniversary of the signing of this pact, 2 million hands clasped each other in solidarity along 600 kilometres of motorway, starting in Tallinn, Estonia, through Latvia's Riga in the middle and all the way down to the Lithuanian capital Vilnius. The protest was a sight to behold: hundreds of thousands of people, from pensioners to children, against a backdrop of long stretches of thick pine forests or city landmarks, holding hands, smiling, waving flags and banners, demanding the end of illegitimate Soviet occupation.

A few weeks later, the Ukrainian journalist and dissident Vyacheslav Chornovil, who'd been in and out of Soviet gulags between 1967 and 1983, founded a civil political party called the People's Movement of Ukraine, abbreviated to Rukh, which literally means 'Movement' in Ukrainian. Rukh was the first opposition party in independent Ukraine. It represented the new civic nationalism, the reclamation of our erased past. Pro-democracy movements in Belarus and the Baltic States, as well as by Crimean Tatars, were closely linked with the rediscovery of national identity. This type of nationalism was a new phenomenon, a thing apart. The followers of these movements did not wish to conquer new territories, instead they wanted to rediscover, preserve and develop all that had been suppressed in their own countries for hundreds of years: their language and all elements of their culture and statehood. It was not ethno-nationalism; it was post-colonial, protective nationalism.

On 21 January 1990, the national movement Rukh organised a protest, inspired by the Baltic Chain. It was called the Ukrainian Wave, or the Chain of Unity, wherein more than a million Ukrainians from every corner of the country formed a human chain stretching from Kyiv to Lviv. I know what January cold in

Ukraine can feel like: it bites and numbs your face and freezes the soles of your feet, even if you stand or walk outside briefly. My heart revs up every time my brain tries to imagine the scale, the togetherness and power of that chain. To stand in that cold, to hold ungloved hands and blue and yellow flags in that cold, along the streets of Ivano-Frankivsk, the tramlines of Lviv, the streets of Chernyhiv and Rivne, and Kyiv arterial roads and squares, created an energy that was unstoppable.

On 11 March 1990, the Supreme Council of the Republic of Lithuania declared the establishment of Lithuanian independence from the Soviet Union. It was the first Soviet republic to claim back its national sovereignty. The Soviets rolled the tanks in, but thousands of unarmed Lithuanians gathered in rallies throughout the country and stood firm.

Seven months later, hundreds of students set up tents in the October Revolution Square in Kyiv (which after that day changed its name to Independence Square) and announced a hunger strike in protest. They, too, wanted a different future. They demanded that the New Union Treaty, a new slightly more democratic union proposed between the fifteen Soviet republics, not be signed, and that the Verkhovna Rada, the Soviet Ukrainian Parliament, be dissolved and democratically re-elected on a multi-party basis. The students kept in mind, and feared, that if Ukraine were to achieve independence like the Baltic States, the old Soviet party bosses would simply change their labels from 'Soviet' to 'independent', the level of corruption remaining the same.

A LESSON ABOUT FREEDOM

It was a chilly October; the students camped out in the cold without eating for two weeks straight. They had water, but they refused to eat or drink anything else, not even sweet tea, until their demands were met. Their action, which was the first Ukrainian maidan – a word that has come to mean public political protest – became known as the Revolution on Granite. They called for the nationalisation of Communist Party property, for early parliamentary elections and the resignation of the head of the Verkhovna Rada, Vitaliy Masol. Not all, but some of the students' demands were met; notably, Vitaliy Masol was forced to resign and Vitold Fokin was appointed as the new prime minister. But the most significant impact of the students' action was to show that political protests were possible, and that they could lead to change.

Fokin was sadly still pro-Soviet, and later part of the so-called Dnipro Clan, a mafia group consisting of oligarchs, ex-Soviet politicians and organised crime figures which kept Ukraine within its grip for years to come. On 24 August 1991, the parliament of the Ukrainian Soviet Socialist Republic, led by Fokin, declared Ukraine independent. Soviet Union bosses in Moscow accepted this on the proviso that the following December there would be an official referendum on independence in Ukraine. You want democracy? Prove it.

I was too young to understand what was happening at that time; besides, I was too focused on my first day at school. The biggest day of my life! I was going to school number 2. In Ukraine, schools were not separated into primary and secondary levels, you attended one big school right the way through, with the children's ages ranging from seven to seventeen. My brother, as well as my cousins Ira (Aunt Zhenia and Uncle Sasha's daughter) and Aliona (Aunt Liuda and Uncle Slava's daughter), all went to school number 2. In fact, Aunt Zhenia was to be my form teacher for the next few years, just as she had been for the others.

Despite the unknown-to-me tribulations within the Soviet Union and the declaration of Ukrainian independence on 24 August, at school number 2 in Khakovka the 1 September ceremony was going ahead as usual. Things had not changed much since my mum and dad were at school: it was still a loud and pompous ceremony, with parents cradling large bouquets swaddled in cellophane. Grandmothers with gold teeth sparkling, eyebrows pencilled in. Grandfathers seated in the front rows, war medals reflecting sunbeams from their lapels. There were still the red kerchiefs blooming on the chests of the older children, the pioneers. And there was no escaping Lenin, nor the banner emblazoned with the usual triple dose of 'Uchitsa!' ('Study!')

All the little girls, including me, were wearing starched white frilly aprons, just as my mother had worn in that photograph from 1966, and huge bows atop their heads. Like the white apron, the bows were requisite uniform for this specific day. For the rest of the year, you could opt out and wear plaits or ponytails tied with elastic bands. The bows were signifiers that we were good and pure, perfect examples of young female socialists; in the years since the Second World War, as the Soviet economy had grown, they had been getting bigger and bigger, a reflected image of national prosperity. By the time I wore them, they were made of white gauze and were huge, like two clouds of cotton candy. I had very long hair, stretching down way below my waist, which meant that Mum had to make two long plaits, then pin them up like pretzels with these two heavy, awkward, scratchy meringues clipped on top. I hated them.

The grand finale of the 1 September ceremony involved one of the youngest girls being given a large iron bell with a red ribbon. The little girl was to be picked up by one of the final-year boys, plonked on his shoulder and paraded around in a big circle, sounding the bell as vigorously as she could. In 1991, that little girl was me. I don't know whether Aunt Zhenia had anything to do with it, in fact I doubt it. I think they picked me because I was the lightest in the class. Younger than the majority of pupils in my class (I'm a July baby), I was knobbly-kneed, scrawny, 20 kilograms at most. Like a small sack of sugar. But when I soared on the shoulder of my cousin's classmate, ringing the heavy bell, watched by everyone, I felt so important. It was my responsibility to announce the new school year open. The local videographer, with his

Stalin-like walrus moustache and clunky camera, was filming me. High up on the older boy's shoulder, I even forgot about the swaying, uncomfortable meringues on my head. Little did I know that this idyllic Soviet show was soon to be over and that the bell I was tolling rang out the death knell of the monstrous regime I was born into.

A few days later, I came out into the school courtyard at lunchtime and saw my Aunt Zhenia talking to the headmaster. I remember that day like it was a dream, a dream so cool and powerful I determined to think about it at least once a month, so I would never forget it.

It may not be the most important thing, but I do want you to picture Aunt Zhenia first, because her look was as unusual and original as her mind. Almost her entire life, she sported a garçon hairstyle that she dyed a then-fashionable henna. As a result, it was the colour of a fresh chestnut with a reddish tinge. It was a short bob, ears exposed, with an asymmetrical long fringe. Because her hair was curly, like my grandmother Liusia's, when it was wet she would pin the longer curls at the front until the hair dried into a 1920s finger wave. She looked unusual among the endless perms and pompadours of the era. She favoured two styles of clothing: either a three-piece suit – a pencil skirt, waistcoat and jacket – or tailored sleeveless dresses worn with an organza or silk blouse, swapped for a polo neck in winter. On 1 September everyone wanted to see what Yevheniia Viktorivna, her full name which she was called at school, would wear. She always had on a new outfit for 1 September, either relying on her husband to procure her something fancy (a chocolate three-piece suit with pearl-cream lining comes to mind), or more often she would sew something herself, such as the off-white suit so chic and elegant that it was talked about in school for months.

Of course, I didn't know she had a style then, but I knew she had authority. We sometimes called her by both names, her full first name – Yevheniia – followed by the patronymic – Viktorivna – even at home. She was strict but fair at school, and at home, within our large extended family, she was adored and respected and listened to. My grandfather Viktor had used a German-sounding word, bayer, to refer to his eldest brother, who took on the role of a parent to him once their parents were dead. Bayer: the eldest son, the second-in-command. Vitya (Viktor Jr), Liusia and Viktor's eldest son, was a bayer. I don't know the word for the female equivalent, if there is one, but Zhenia was that. She was the matriarch's second-in-command and, being the oldest daughter, she had helped Liusia to hold everything together and to look after her younger siblings, Valentina, Slava, Yura and the baby of the family, my mum, Olga.

That dream day in the courtyard at school, I came out of the long corridor after the bell rang for us to take a break. I stood on the step of the porch looking longingly towards the cafeteria building across the courtyard, where, had I not forgotten my pocket money, I would now be going to get my much-desired novelty lunch. There was a whole new craze in town called pizza! (Except now, looking back, I realise it was in fact enriched local pyrizhky bun dough, slightly flattened, with an indentation for a small, ambrosial puddle of Marie Rose sauce and chopped sosysky, the frankfurter-style processed sausage.)

I looked around. The girls were using skipping ropes or playing rezinochky: 'elastics'. I didn't have friends yet, so I stood, unsure. I was bad at elastics, and I was bad at ropes, and even hopscotch was not my forte. But here was Zhenia — or in that moment most definitely Yevheniia Viktorivna — talking to the headmaster. She faced in my direction but she did not see me. Their voices got louder and louder; I pricked up my ears, while pretending I was looking elsewhere. Not that they would have noticed me anyway, they were too involved in their conversation. Yevheniia Viktorivna raised her voice, or not raised exactly, as her voice was not shouty or shrill. Rather, her voice gradually filled, expanded, got bigger and more resolute. I couldn't see the headmaster's face, only his back. He was very tall and thin, like a pencil in his black suit, I thought. As she spoke, my aunt's arms moved in unison with her words, the silk of her sleeves shimmering and floating up and down, up and down, like a sail, or like the waves themselves.

And suddenly she stopped and I heard her say, very clearly, definitively: 'My children will NOT be Oktobrists.' She was talking about the next big event in the school calendar, the celebration of the October 1917 revolution, the day when all first-years were sworn in to become Oktiabriata, little Oktobrists. Two years later, we would be pioneers. The famous red kerchief would be tied around our necks and we would solemnly swear to be model Communist citizens. We would swear to study hard, we would swear to be kind, and we would swear to always tell the truth and nothing but the truth.

The headmaster mumbled, telling my aunt that Antonovna, the teacher from the parallel class, planned to do it. But Yevheniia Viktorivna said, 'Well, she can fall off a cliff if she likes, but MY children will not be Oktiabriata.' And then, loud and clear, 'It's over!' And again, just in case, 'My children will not be Oktiabriata!'

I stood there and watched them both. They must have pivoted during their talk, or perhaps I sneakily walked to a different spot, I cannot recall, but what I do remember is seeing the headmaster's face. He had a rather long face and I thought, 'He looks like a stunned horse.' He shrivelled into himself like a dry leaf under my black lacquered shoe. Yevheniia's cut-glass cheekbones, fierce violet-blue eyes and the down-turned corners of her mouth, just like Mum's and mine, looked even more striking. Her wavy chestnut bob swayed another definitive 'no' and, at least in my mind, she clenched her fists and stomped her foot.

My feelings were very mixed. On the one hand, it was so utterly prykolno, 'cool', to see my aunt, my teacher, stand her ground so fearlessly in front of the head of school. And on the other, my stomach felt like it was eating itself. That sinking feeling, the dead butterflies. I realised that I would never walk in a line wearing the red kerchief, the beacon of responsibility. Or would I?

No. I would not. Yevheniia Viktorivna kept her word. We were the only class in the whole town that shunned the ceremony in October. We did not become Oktiabriata. Six weeks later, on 1 December, 90.32 per cent of Ukrainians voted to leave the USSR. Zhenia urged the whole extended family, all friends, colleagues and acquaintances, to vote for Chornovil's Rukh. Verkhovna Rada – the Ukrainian parliament – declared the Independence of Ukraine. This time irreversibly.

When I ask Iryna to tell me more about her mother, Aunt Zhenia, she says, 'Apart from language, and you know she campaigned locally for the change in education methodology and language, Mum was saturated with the idea of Ukrainian statehood.' Chornovil was her idol. She was not an official member of the Rukh movement, but she adhered to Chornovil's post-colonial nationalism.

Iryna reminds me that Zhenia, like her and Mum's oldest brother Uncle Viktor, had been born in wartime. Viktor Jr was born in March 1942, nine months after Viktor Sr retreated with the Soviet Army before the Nazis. Aunt Zhenia was born in August 1944, nine months after the Third Ukrainian Front made its fateful advance. They both remembered the tough post-war years, the starvation, the repressions, Viktor's imprisonment, living in the annexe at their grandmother Liza's, Stalin's death. Both became fiercely political and patriotic. The Ukrainian word for 'cheers', when a toast is made, is budmo, which means 'let us be' or 'we shall be'. And this is how Zhenia felt.

It was her mission, the main purpose of her life, not just to educate, but to do the opposite of what the Soviets had done to us. She taught us not to take things at face value and certainly not doggedly to obey authority, but to question and to reason. She was the type of teacher who would have given Dad a five plus for his essay on *Fantômas*, even with all his sloppy grammatical mistakes. She believed in rewarding independent thought and encouraged us to think for ourselves every single day. She even introduced traditional embroidery classes in her lessons, a surprise hit among many of the boys. It steadied our brains, forced us to be in the present, while the finished pieces brought us closer to traditional Ukrainian culture as well as giving us a sense of accomplishment.

Zhenia's ally at school was a history teacher called Viktor Zubkov. My school years were a time – after Ukraine's independence, as the countries of Eastern Europe all found their freedom – when even more secrets came out, the scope of Soviet repressions revealed to be so much bigger than anyone thought. The Great Hush was over and history was unravelling like a strip of orange peel coming off the fruit, each segment tasted and digested in a new way. We talked of land-lease, we talked of Chernobyl. Tall, with big expressive eyes and a wicked sense of humour, Zubkov taught us all, Iryna, my brother and me. And we loved him. He was our favourite teacher. I remember one time he took our whole class to an ancient burial mound in Kherson and he knighted us with an old musket, both boys and girls, to become Cossacks. We were high up on a hill covered by tall wild grasses. I remember the sun spilling across the steppe, the breeze coming from the Dnipro that looked like the sea. And most of all I remember the pride that I felt. I, a girl, was to become a real Cossack. A warrior!

Mum and Dad did not keep any of our childhood mementos such as drawings, but, somehow, stuck between their letters from the 1970s, I found a history essay, which I wrote aged ten. The topic was unusual. We were to write about what we liked about our history lessons, and to give examples. I described a recent lesson where Zubkov asked us a trick question in class, something that we all rushed to answer without thinking. When he revealed, with a stab of a wink, that we were all wrong, even his son Andriy, my classmate, we exploded in raucous protestations, roaring that it was unfair. In my essay, I say that I enjoyed this moment the most, the fun of being tricked like this and to be taught to pause and to think and to challenge my own thoughts. It was a lesson about considering different options; a lesson ultimately about the plasticity of the mind; a lesson about freedom.

At school, Zhenia and Zubkov both pushed us to develop a questioning, analytical mind, and that's what I wanted to do, to compare personal accounts of my family with what was written in history books. I was trying to stitch together the stories I heard at home with what had happened in the wider embroidery of history. History books elaborated on what had happened to my family: the disturbing bits my relatives left out of their stories to spare me were all there, the horror and injustice encoded within each letter of Holodomor, gulag, executions, massacres, sexual violence.

The stories told by my grandmother Liusia or snippets of wartime experience from my grandfather Viktor had been hard to make sense of. I never doubted that they were true, not even for a second, but as I got older, I needed books to help me join the dots. Ukrainian independence had brought these truths to the fore. Before Ukraine's independence, history was doctored. By the time I was studying history in the 1990s, Stalinist repressions and Holodomor were discussed, Lenin was no longer on the last remaining pedestal as the eternal leader (even though his statue, hand outstretched towards Dnipro, stood opposite the music school in Kakhovka until 2014). So my grandparents' stories were corroborated. School history and my home history finally matched.

Numerous times, I have imagined grandfather Viktor boarding a train from the Russian military town of Balashov to Kyiv in June 1941, straight after the Germans invaded the USSR. It is easy to imagine him physically, as there is a portrait of him wearing military uniform, taken on conscription. His eyes are almost transparent in the sepia photograph, his hair the colour of scorched summer grass, swept back and glossy. I wonder what he felt like, boarding that train, what his thoughts were on the way.

Now here I am in 2022, talking to my brother, a soldier, like Viktor. I think of my grandmother Vera's toast, 'The main thing is that there is no war,' a flare of urgency followed by sadness in her eyes and voice every single time after raising a glass of her homemade wine. I think how not one generation of my family has escaped war. 'Sash, your camera must not be working. I can see myself, I can hear you, but I can't see you at all.' 'No no, the camera is on. They just switched off the electricity.'

I am in my garden, on a bench, the spot that catches the last rays of the day. My sunset is two hours behind Ukraine's. A little square of my face is scrunched up in the light of the sunset, facing the pitch-black of the screen on the other side. I take a screenshot, lest I ever forget this moment. Me, peaceful sunset; Sash, wartime blackout. Later, when I look back at it, I can just about make out the faded porcelain of Sasha's sclera, the UK light reflected in the apple of my brother's eye. I ask Sasha the difficult questions. About what happened during and after 22 February, two days before the invasion, when Putin made his intentions clear and Kyivans realised they needed to leave in earnest, and quickly. I had thought he, too, was going to leave the city. He said, yes that had been his plan; he put his clothes in the large suitcase with those of his sons, they were ready to leave for Lviv. 'And then, you know, I saw the video footage of the tanks rolling around Kyiv. I saw the footage of the tank rolling over somebody's car with a person inside it.' I saw it too, it knocked me out for a few days, I could not understand it with my brain, what was happening, how was it possible?

'It made me think clearly,' Sasha says. 'I thought, how do you imagine life for yourself in the future? What comes next? Do we give up Kyiv? All the Russians coming to live in people's apartments and houses? And you know, would I torture myself for the rest of my life, that I did nothing to help the situation? I couldn't do it, I doubt I could keep living and working somewhere else. And even less to stay here and accept them, the world they bring here. In that scenario, you lose everything. If they win, this is it. You own nothing, you are nobody here on your own land, and you are called Nothing. You lose your very name. They would erase our self-identification, grind our minds and our will into sawdust, like they did before. I could never just slot into the new system, the russki mir.' I think how mir means both 'peace' and 'world' in Russian. 'World peace' all in one word. The Russian world, the Russian peace. Systema: a set-up.

Sasha's voice jolts me out of my thoughts, spills out of the darkness. 'I thought, if I do not do anything, they will kill me later anyway. So I might as well do something. And then I realised that to join the territorial forces I did not need any special training. I could simply volunteer. I quietly took my clothes out of the large suitcase before we left our apartment, I walked my sons down, but I didn't get in the car myself. I told them my plan there and then and waved them goodbye.' I had not known these details, so we keep silent for a few beats, and then I ask him, 'What happened next?'

'I was ready. So I woke up, at 6 a.m., but it was too early, they hadn't opened yet, the centres where you enrol for territorial defence. The city was empty. Some areas of Kyiv, like the one I lived in, were already at capacity and did not accept any more volunteers. But the Shevchenko area still did, so I rushed there.' 'Tell me again what kinds of Kyivans joined with you?' I ask. 'Olia, the city was suddenly empty. A lot of men were taking their families out, which was a good thing to do, but loads went to volunteer too. There were queues, waiting lists! Anyway, Anton is an IT guy, we still work together. Nastya is a choreographer, but she worked at a university, remember she is the one I told you who showed up at work on day two after the invasion.' He lets out a short laugh, he loves Nastya's determination. Then he continues, 'You know Borysovich of course, he used to do refurbishments, apartments, but he also did military service in his youth, he had experience, so he was given a higher rank straight away. You know Akhtem Seitablaiev, the Crimean Tatar director. Mmmm, there was another guy, such a nice guy, Pasha! His friends, his neighbours, did military service when they were young, so he offered to give them a lift to the recruitment centre. And then when he dropped them off, he suddenly decided to join too. People from all

A LESSON ABOUT FREEDOM

walks of life, actors, films and theatre, and remember the guy who came to London last year? The bandura player, Kompanitenko, he toured around the UK last year. Yeaaaaah, he is still with us.'

We are both quiet for a bit and then we lose the connection. I wait for him. I think of Vera again, 'The main thing is that there is no war, eh babul'ka Vera.'

'... Sorry my generator, and the power bank, everything overheated. I'm back. Anyway, Ol', I wanted to fight so my sons don't have to. Even... so our grandchildren don't have to, Olia. Yours and mine and everybody's. Because if we miss this moment, we will never close this circle.'

I mention Viktor, our grandfather, and the Battle for Kyiv of 1941. Sasha does not know this story, so I recap, and tell him about the Irpin River. The thin sheet of ice on its waters, the unusual freezing cold in September, the bullets released into thick clumps of bullrushes. How Viktor hid in the reeds and how he sat there for days, in the water. How he got captured.

And Sasha exclaims, 'This is where I was, Olichka! It was March. Mum's birthday. The Russians had taken Bucha and Hostomel, and this river, Irpin River, it was between us, us and the enemy. They were on the other side, but they couldn't cross the water. Seven times they tried to throw pontoons over and seven times the Ukrainian artillery beat them off. We thought that there was a load of us, but there were indeed very few of us. We were lucky, Ol', LU-CKY. They thought they were rolling into Kyiv, straight to a welcome parade with open arms clutching flowers. But there was no parade and they did not organise their logistics.' He tells a long story. I listen as if he is telling me a fairytale. Like it is one of Dad's tales of adventure from when we were small.

'It was by the forest, at the end of the tram station, we hid behind a concrete tram stop, by a small café. And then I see something like fireworks, fireworks that move rapidly towards me. And I shout up into the air: "This is Grady!!!!"' (Grad literally means 'hail' and is a Russian weapons system.) 'They discovered our positions!' He catches his breath. 'Behind us a private house blew up, you know this suburban area is affluent, the houses there are very nice.' 'Was it loud, Sash?' 'Yeah, of course. So it started banging, and it felt like it took only a few seconds to orientate ourselves, we learned very quickly to differentiate how close they were falling to us or how far away they were. And I remember pure clarity. I was not panicked, I listened very intently and was very much in the moment. But also, you know, I had a hundred thousand thoughts rushing through my head. It was interesting, looking back. It was only a couple of minutes, this attack, but it was…' '… The thing they say about your life flashing before your eyes in seconds?' 'Yes, exactly. Time and space were warped and twisted. Time slowed down in an extreme way, unlike anything I had experienced before. So I remember all of these thoughts.'

Sasha's voice slows down, and he elongates all his vowels as he speaks, as if to emphasise just how much careful philosophising and soul-searching he was able to do at the same time as listening out for the hailing missiles. 'I was thinking, whyyyyy do I live this way…? If I survive this, I will change this this this and thiiiiis.' He swears, he is still there with missiles flying over his head. 'Bliaaaaad, and today is Mum's biiiiirthday. And if I survive, I will…' The line interrupts briefly. And then he's back, mid-sentence… 'And then very close it banged, and you know it felt like a little bit of the zemelka, of the soil you know, prysypala.' He uses the diminutive word zemelka, 'little earth', and prysypala, 'sprinkled', and it sounds tender and understated. The earth lightly sprinkled him. 'And I think, meh OK, a little bit of soil. In the morning we went back. And then I noticed I had a hole in my trousers. I thought, shit, when did I manage to rip the new uniform trousers… I looked at my thigh and saw that it was already closed, the gash had sealed over, the blood was caked dry. And then I remembered the sprinkling of the earth. Must have been a little bit of shrapnel,' he says. 'So yeah… a funny story.'

Crimean Tatars in Gurzuf in Crimea

7

Asret[1]

In July 2022, three months after my parents fled Kakhovka, I finally persuade them to come to England. I want to take them to Devon. They need to breathe. To breathe fresh air and smell their grandchildren's heads. My parents were changed, but they hadn't lost hope that they would be able to return to Ukraine soon enough. They did not accept that terrible word: exile. That word was for history books and historical novels. And even though Mum's own mother Liusia and father Viktor had once been exiles, I never associated this word with the stories they shared.

---

[1] Asret means 'exile' in Crimean Tatar, or Qırımlı.

I found a holiday cottage for us ten minutes away from the sea, a cosy-looking place with an elaborate little garden at the front. We are met on arrival by a narrow stone path and a huge globe artichoke plant. The artichoke was blooming, nectar-rich violet flowers ripe for the bees' dinner. To the left, two little signs read 'thyme' and 'dill'. The dill plant turns out to be fennel, but the fact that the owner wanted their fennel to be dill is comforting to us. Dill is life, I often say, we use it in almost every savoury dish. There is a mighty bay shrub and a small Japanese maple, its leaves rusty-red. A wattle tree looks like the wild olives from the shores of the River Dnipro, which is also a comfort.

I took a photograph of Mum that first day, down by the sea, where we sat for a long time under the cliff, staring into a rock pool. The ripples on the water are so gentle, like a box-pleated skirt or the open bellows of an accordion. The rocks behind her sweep to the right and on the bias; you can almost hear the jaunty clank of earthquakes, ancient and ghostly. Her body creates angular dynamics, with one foot on an algae-sprayed rock and the other just above as she leans away from the hill towards the sea and points at something far in the distance. She is wearing a gauzy smock patterned with burgundy and azure lion fish. Her mouth is frozen in a pointed 'O', brows furrowed, but you know she is happy and excited. She was so alive that day, almost manic with joy and wonder.

Mum says she had a dream the night before, in our London house. She describes it in that special ragged tone of voice which we reserve for subjects such as these, when we know in advance that the dream is of a type we often share. 'Ty znayesh, yak filmy.' 'You know this sort, like the movies.' They are cinematic dreams, the dreams that feel real. She says a white tiger's paws had landed softly on her shoulder blades. The tiger is grunting and breathing heavily into the nape of her neck, pushing Mum forward, forcing her to take little steps. She does not feel fear, but she is aware that, if she panics, the tiger will sense the adrenaline brushing his nostrils and will tear her apart. Then she spots two doors: two choices. She chooses the correct door and wakes up.

It is the morning of 23 July, our third day there; when I come back to the cottage after spending the morning walking, I see Mum's ashen face. Her beach-day energy, from the time spent on those algae-green rocks two days before, is now a ghost from a distant past. She moves around the tiled kitchen, mopping it, she tends to the boiling pot of soup, she avoids eye contact and I know she's been cleaning for hours. 'Mama, are you OK? What happened?' Her face scrunches like a dried apricot. Kolya had called. Kolya has been working for my parents for more than twenty years, helping around the house; we love him like a friend. He decided to stay in Kakhovka and, when my parents left, Dad asked him to move into the house, or at least to stay there from time to time, to keep an eye on things, maybe tend to the garden.

On the call, Kolya had said that 'polite green men' had visited our house and demanded the keys. They announced they would be living there… temporarily. They magnanimously said if there were computers there, or anything else valuable, to take them out.

'Where is Tato, Mama? Upstairs?' I am glad that the staircase is covered in carpet; it muffles my normally heavy steps and I don't want them to sound menacing as I walk upstairs. I find Dad buried in the safety of the billowing duvet, hidden in the meringue comfort of its warmth. It looks like the duvet has swallowed him whole. 'Dad, are you asleep?' 'Niet, dochenka.' I sit at the bottom of the bed and wait.

Mum comes in and sits beside me on the bed. She is crying as she always cries: soundlessly, face elongated in an attempt to keep it under control. I try to make a joke. 'At least it's not the roaming crew from *The Road*. Maybe they won't shit all over the carpets?'

And that comment reminded me about the Brezhnev rug. I don't know where Dad got it, he doesn't either. In the early 1990s it was common, when an old Soviet relic was unearthed, either to resell it to foreigners (as my teenage brother did) or to keep it as a memento. This rug was such a historical relic. It was hand-woven by the people of Tajikistan and the makers had woven into it: 'From the people of Tajikistan to Comrade Brezhnev'. Above the Russian writing loomed a perfect facsimile of Brezhnev's face. We kept the rug, as we liked to walk all over it, and it was in my parents' bedroom. I thought to myself, 'Will the intruders think we were staunch Soviets? Will this mean they might spare the house? Or will they get wasted on

Dad's gin and whisky and kiss Brezhnev's lips in a drunken stupor?'

Mum and I get under the duvet, next to Dad. We lie silently together. Mum keeps her head down, dark circles cradling her eyes like two half-moons. Dad's face is still hidden behind the duvet, but I squeeze his wrist and feel his pulse on my fingers: it's fast, but I know he won't cry. We may never see our home again. We will definitely never see it as we remember it.

'If we stayed, I don't think they would have come to claim the house,' Dad says. A pause. 'But I am certain that I would have visited one of the basements already.' V podval, 'to the basement' in Russian. People who remained in occupied territories, those who resisted, often disappeared, sometimes for days, sometimes months; some are still missing. There are reports of basements, grim, unofficial interrogation centres, some of them are outright torture chambers. I doubt they would have tortured my dad, but I don't think he would have had a ball either, had he remained. He was correct, he definitely would have been interrogated. After all, they knew that his son, Sasha, was now in the Ukrainian military.

Mum phones Kolya and asks him to hide the expensive china. She packed all the things that had sentimental value into Dad's car when they fled: the photos and the embroideries and the letters. What is it that remains? The little collection of Swarovski figurines? The tiny piano and the inkpot with a delicate golden quill, the tiny hedgehog and the parasol, all arranged carefully on the cabinet? Or was it another collection? Was it the decorative plates – Mum's holiday trophies – that hung on the wall? Rugs? The Czech chandelier from the living room, with the dazzling crystals? The good reproductions of famous oil paintings by that artist from Kherson?

I try to imagine what the impostors in our house are feeling. What are they like? What do they say when they phone their wives? 'These ukropy [dill heads] don't just have a washing machine, but also a dishwasher! They have a sauna and a steam room! They have a Japanese garden, an orchard and a pine forest, a huge pond!' My mind races. Will they feel the love and care that went into the garden? Will they understand the work that went into it all? Would they care? Shall I try to speak to them, to call them? 'Get the fuck out of our house!'

The next morning, I come into my parents' bedroom. Dad has his iPad on his belly, Mum is listening to Duolingo Italiano. Mum's neat little papers, with hand-written words she'd learnt, flutter around her like delicate, pale metelyky ('moths'). I ask to squeeze in. I want to feel like a child again, and I want them to feel like parents. 'Tatous, how's things?' 'I spoke to Kolya and then to Vadim [Dad's nephew, who lives in Voznesensk]. They have installed some satellites on our roof. I told Vadim to get the exact coordinates and if they put something important there, like a tank, I will tell the ZSU to strike it.'

I remember Dad's Armenian aunt Tamara often told us about their house in Karabakh, which they were forced to leave behind when the war broke out with Azerbaijan in the late 1980s. I will never forget the time when Nina, Tamara's daughter, described seeing the house many years later, derelict, the books in one of their big rooms, the library – the pride of the family – crumpled and speckled with mould, pages stuck together, flapping in the wind in scraggy clumps, one of the saddest things she'd ever seen. I think of other stories of exile and return. But mostly, I think of Crimean friends and their families, their story a mirror of the past that leads into our future.

The people of Crimea are my family's historical siblings. It is a mere 75 kilometres from my hometown of Kakhovka to the Crimean peninsula, the same distance that Milton Keynes is from London. We are also connected to it by history. From the fourteenth century, my native region of Kherson was part of the Crimean Khanate, and since the 1950s the two regions have been linked by the umbilical cord that is the North Crimean Canal. The canal pumps fresh water into Crimea, without which it is impossible to water and feed the population that it hosts today, or for the chemical plants to operate safely. Despite its proximity and the physical and historical connection, Crimean history, shamefully, remained little known to me until Crimea was taken away.

But because it was so close, we visited often. There is a video of my family and me on holiday there from the summer of 1989. I remember that holiday. On the short journey from Kakhovka to the Crimean border, my brother, grandmother Vera – still sprightly and loud – and I engaged in our regular entertainment, a card game called Durak (a Russian word with Turkic origins, meaning 'Fool'), in the back of Dad's milk-coloured Lada. It felt like the sun was melting the pockmarked road, punctuated by vanishing puddle-like mirages. Dark, patterned curtains at the back of the car were failing to protect us from the sweltering heat, the air was stifling. There were no motorways, just a single carriageway. Everyone drove at more than 70 kilometres an hour anyway, swerving around each other dangerously; we Ukrainians were used to living on the edge.

The first stretch of the journey was boring, it was flat and familiar, so we entertained ourselves as best we could. 'Koroooool!' my grandmother would shout out during our card game, making sure to emphasise that second 'o', like it held all the complete and destructive power of her 'King'. She would win again and again, thrashing us and occasionally offering to lose on purpose (we would refuse, with dignity). We would laugh and take a break from the card game to play another: Spot the Car, point out all the white Volgas (a rarity), all the dusty, milky Ladas (more effort as there were so many), until the road turned into a snake and the landscape changed from flat and arid to steep and covered in exotic trees. Along the road, people were selling flat peaches and their allium counterparts: flat red onions, a Crimean speciality. But, once we finally saw the huge laccolith mountain – the landmark that told us we were nearly there – our attention was fully diverted to the scene outside the car window. The mountain which looked like a giant animal sipping from the edge of the shore into the Black Sea.

As kids, we only knew the Russian moniker for it: Medved Gora. Only as an adult did I find out that the mountain's original local name in Greek antiquity would have been Κριοῦ μέτωπον (Kriou Metopon), 'Ram's Head'. From around the thirteenth century, it was called by its Crimean Tatar (Qırımlı) name: Ayu-Dağ, 'Bear Mountain'. The bear's head (and I agree with the Qırımlı name, as it looks more like a bear than a ram) was right in the smooth waters of the Black Sea. Its back was covered in the hide of fluffy oak trees and, as a kid, I liked to imagine that all the animals that lived in his hide were the fleas on the bear. Boars, foxes, deer, martens, lizards, even the cormorants and jays and owls, hopping among the jasmine and juniper shrubs, pausing, burrowing through the soil of the bear's dandruff and giving his skin a nibble. In my mind's eye, the bear would lift his head and, almost in slow motion because of his size, would turn it towards his curved spine, scratching with his giant alabaster teeth where it itched from the tiny bites. Then he would go back to slurping at the gentle spume of the sea. 'A drink at last!' I always thought.

A local folkloric tale about the Ayu-Dağ goes like this. Many moons ago, a giant bear trundled through the forests of Crimea. Exhausted from the long walk, he found himself in Partenit Valley. This was long before the valley was called Partenit, perhaps even before the time when it was called Parthenium, and certainly it was long before it was filled with the gnarled edges of vine plants and pink-cheeked pistachio groves. It was salty-wild and bountiful and the bear decided to stay there forever. The bear was parched and he rushed to the water, but the God of the Sea spotted how huge the bear was and feared that the beast would empty out the sea, so he turned him into stone. Another version about Ayu-Dağ tells the story of a bear who fell in love with a girl and kept her against her will for hundreds of years. But one day, the girl spotted a passing ship sailing by, made a fire and attracted its attention with the wisp and whorl of the smoke. Having lost his captive, the bear pined for her so long that he finally turned to stone out of grief.

But, during those childhood family trips with Vera, I knew nothing of the bear's thirst for the whole of the inhospitable sea, or for his love of the captured girl. In that homemade family holiday video from 1989, we cannot see Dad, as he is filming, but there are the rest of us in our fantastic outfits. Vera looks moody in her paisley-patterned button-front dress. Her mouth glistens with gold teeth, her soft neck adorned with her inevitable horseshoe pendant, its arch framing a fleshy skin-coloured birthmark on her chest. I always loved staring at both: the horseshoe and the birthmark. I thought that both — the flesh and the gold surrounding it — were sources of limitless luck. My brother is thirteen going on seventeen, wearing red tracksuit trousers, narrow at the ankles, a black bum bag around his strong waist, black sliders on his feet and no top. His wiry, muscular torso is all brushed bronze against the chipped sky-blue promenade railing, faded lavender skies and sea. Mum's tan is so dark that her face is lost within the shade of her light straw hat. Her curly ponytail is jet black, her ears are clipped with aquamarine earrings, her eyes — the same colour as the earrings — burst out of her bronzed face, her lips 1980s fuchsia.

And finally there is me, running after Vera, pretending to know how to tell the time from my brand-new watch. I have short baby shark teeth, a gummy smile and a pug nose. I am wearing a white T-shirt with a tennis racket on it and the word Тенис in Russian written underneath, a pink-rimmed sailor's hat and — la pièce de résistance — The Shorts. They are a patchwork of an American flag with WASHINGTON running down each leg in capital letters. We don't know if we bought them with the rest of the nautical outfit right there in Aluşta (Alushta), or if my dad bought them for me in Odesa at one of the famous tolkuchkas. (Tolkuchka comes from the Russian word tolkat, 'to shove'. It is, essentially, a busy flea-market with the crowds attracted by second-hand clothing from abroad, which at the time still had an association with the good life that we were so desperate to experience.)

In the video, we are hitting all the attractions, hovering around the Rotunda – a 1951 faux Grecian arch – Aluşta's main Soviet landmark. On it we see the original engraving: Трудящиеся имеют право на отдых, 'Workers have the right to leisure'. You can say that again. When I look at the video now, it is so obvious that everyone in it is either Russian or Ukrainian. We were, of course, walking in the most touristy part of the city. But where were the Crimean Tatars, one of the indigenous nations of the peninsula?

The Crimean peninsula has an ancient, multicultural history, a perpetual broth of civilisations, new ingredients added over time. It has been inhabited by Tauri (Scythian) tribes, Cimmerians, Sarmatians, and also by Greeks, Romans, Venetians and Genoese, Huns and Goths. Early visitors had found it difficult to settle, what with its dry land and inhospitable sea. However, around the thirteenth century, a group did manage to make a settlement, a group that became known as 'Crimean Tatars' or, recently and more authentically, as the Qırımlı.

The Russian Empire made numerous attempts at annexation, but Qırımlı kept electing khans who were anti-Russian and sided with their natural ally and trading partner, Ottoman Turks. In 1783, the army of the Russian Empire under Catherine the Great invaded and largely cleared Crimea for Russians. Many of the Crimean Tatars who refused to assimilate to Russian culture were sent into exile in Turkey, while Crimean Greeks and Armenians were booted out to the Azov Sea area, modern-day Mariupol in Ukraine. The trauma and genocide began not with Stalin but with Catherine. By 1941 when the Germans occupied Crimea, the population remained 68 per cent Crimean Tatar, with most of the men, about 20,000 of them, fighting in the Red Army. On 10 May 1944, Lavrentiy Beria and Stalin falsely accused the entire Crimean nation of collaboration with the occupying Nazi army. On 18 May 1944, in the early hours, a three-day deportation began. This was only six years after my great-grandmother – herself deported to Russia's northern Vologda, near to Finland, by the Soviets – finally managed to return from exile to Ukraine with her five surviving children, including my grandmother Liusia.

Accounts of the Crimean deportation make them sound just as cruel as that of my grandmother. Almost every account of that night goes like this. In the house, there is a woman sleeping with her children and often the elderly. The father is away, still fighting the Germans. At around 5 a.m., the Soviets barge in and wake everyone up. This is standard practice: aggressive uniformed men barging in on a family when they're disorientated and at their most vulnerable. The horse and the cow can sense the danger and commotion and make a racket. The family has fifteen minutes to get ready, they are instructed not to take anything with them. Because it is so sudden and aggressive, some think they are being taken to be executed. Some grab a little flour or water, or remnants of the previous night's dinner, and stuff them into a bag.

People are taken to the cemetery or the centre of the village. American lease Studebakers are now used in a different way to how my grandfather Viktor used them. They serve as transport for Crimean Tatar families who are taken to the train station. There is chaos. People are panicking. Freight trains await. The freight trains are not adapted for transporting humans. Families, at gun point, are shoved into the train wagons; some are forcibly torn apart, not allowed to travel together. In February, those same trains had been used to transport – in a similar inhumane way – the people of the Caucasus: the Muslims – Chechens, Karachay, Dagestanis and the Buddhist Kalmyks. Blood and faeces remain in the wagons from that previous deportation.

People do not know where they are being taken, nobody tells them anything at all. They travel for an average of eighteen days. There is no food, no toilets. People die, there isn't enough air. At each stop the soldiers pass by every carriage and shout, 'Any dead?' Sometimes no answer comes because the whole wagon has become a coffin. They simply drag the bodies out and leave them in ditches by the side of the tracks.

Sixteen thousand Greeks, nearly 10,000 Armenians, and 12,600 Bulgarians were deported together with the Crimean Tatars. Out of the 180,000 Crimean Tatars that were on the peninsula at the time, around 150,000 were deported to the Uzbek Socialist Soviet Republic (SSR); 8,500 to Mariupol, and more than 4,000 to the Kazakh SSR; the remaining were sent to various remote regions of the Russian Soviet Federative Socialist Republic (SFSR). Wherever the deported were eventually dumped, the conditions they found were desperate. The local populations were not prepared. There was no shelter, no food, disease spread. It is said that 110,000 people died as a result of the deportation, roughly 46 per cent of the Crimean population.

As soon as the Crimean Tatar people had been deported, the Russian invaders began carefully erasing their history and culture, like lines of graphite pencil with a rubber. The monuments which recalled the Tatar presence were either destroyed or appropriated. Books written by Crimean Tatars were removed from library shelves and some were burnt; all references to Crimean Tatars in existing history books, if there were any, were taken out. As early as 1945, place names on the peninsula were Russified. On 25 July 1946, Crimea was reduced to the status of an oblast, forming part of the Russian Soviet Federative Socialist Republic. Tatars were gone, their traces erased.

After Stalin's death in 1953, most of the deported were allowed to return to their homes. The only three groups that were denied this right were Crimean Tatars, Volga Germans and Meskhetian Turks (Turks who lived in the territory of Georgia). They were to remain in exile indefinitely. It's true that they no longer had to be confined to barbed-wire-fence settlements or to report regularly to the authorities, like prisoners on parole, so some of their civic rights were rehabilitated, but returning to Crimea remained forbidden. In the 1970s, a few Crimean Tatars tried to sneak back in, disguised as tourists, some to merely glimpse their lost homeland, others trying to remain there (whose attempts were unsuccessful). It was not until the late 1980s that they were officially allowed to return. But even throughout the early 1990s, Crimean Tatars were denied accommodation in their traditional places of settlement. Instead, they were forced to set up refugee camps in the arid steppe, far away from life-giving water.

That water, most of which comes from the North Crimean Canal, from Ukraine, flows through Ukraine's arteries to reach Crimea's veins.

The year before the war started, in 2021, I was in Edinburgh on a book tour, speaking about my latest cookbook. That evening, I spotted a young couple in the audience. The woman's face drew me in especially; it felt familiar and she seemed to recognise my stories. After the talk, the couple came up to me. 'We are Ukrainian,' they said. The woman explained further: 'Well, I was born in Tajikistan,' she said. 'But Crimea is my homeland.' Her name was Silvia. She was half-Crimean Tatar, half-Tajik. She told me that, after eventually returning to Crimea in the late 1990s, most of her family had to flee again in 2014 after Russia annexed the peninsula. We hugged and exchanged emails and words of hope and support. We were both aware of the build-up of Russian troops by the borders of Ukraine, which had already started even then.

Silvia gave me the phone numbers of her mum and aunt, and after my parents had lost their home to the polite green men, I decided to get in touch. I wanted to hear more of the family's story. Could I learn something from them that might make my parents' ordeal of exile more manageable and not entirely devoid of hope? This is what I learned.

Susanna Zakir, Silvia's aunt by marriage, visited her historical homeland of Crimea for the first time in 1992. Like all Crimean Tatars of her generation, she was born in exile – in Tajikistan, Central Asia – in the early 1960s. She remembers the family elders referred to Crimea as Yeshi Ada, 'The Green Isle', the land of longing. Even though her homeland, as her parents knew it, was missing from books and movies, she was familiar with her father's native village through his pencil-on-paper sketches. The language, the memories, the love of gardening and nature were passed on to those born in exile, including Susanna; their desire to return to their paradise lost kept alight by those who survived the forced deportation.

Susanna moved to Crimea in 1992 and settled near Feodosiya. She went to visit her father's home, but the owner would not let her in. The second time Susanna went to visit her father's home was in 2013. This time she took her 24-year-old daughter Ediye. They were determined to find her father's village. They got on the bus in the coastal town of Aluşta (Alushta), where I had holidayed with my family in 1989, wearing those flea market American flag shorts. The bus swerved up the side of a steep mountain, a narrow dusty switchback of a road, coughing up thousands of aromatic particles from herbs, wildflowers, pine needles. Apple, fig and almond trees shimmered in the morning sun. When they arrived, Susanna recognised the alleys flanked by tall cypress trees from her father's pencil sketches. In both the stories and drawings of her father, cypresses held a very special place. She finally understood why when she saw them. They were everywhere. Planted by the villagers along the alleys to make the village look beautiful hundreds of years ago, now they looked lonely, the sentinels of sorrow. That feeling of longing, which Qırımlı call asret, lived within the trunks of these cypress trees.

When they got off the bus, the name Yeşil Ada (Yeshil Ada), the Green Island, made perfect sense. The landscape was macerated in concentrated shades of green. The village itself seemed to be embraced by green; even the lake looked emerald, reflecting the elms and pine trees on its edges. Behind the thick layer of trees they saw mountain peaks peeping right above, greeting them. Little paths went up the mountain, splitting into other paths, like veins on a vine leaf. Susanna wanted to paint it all. No more subdued pencil sketches; the colours could finally be summoned.

But first she had to find her father Amza's house. They did not know the address, so they decided to follow the memory of her father's sketches and their guts. They did know – they had managed to find out just a little information – that the house was being lived in by a teacher called Arife. They thought, if they didn't find the house, at least they would see the village from up high. Slowly, they set off, breathing in deeply the heady punch of pine resin, cow dung, dry herbaceous soil, the roses planted by every single house and the smell of water... They walked up, comparing each pine to the pencilled pines from the drawings, led by both to where they needed to go. Finally, they reached gates on a curve of the road, and something – a feeling – told them to stop. They stood there wondering whether to knock or to wait for someone passing by. Then a group of young locals passed. 'Meraba!' ('Greetings!') 'We are looking for Arife's house.' 'You are standing in front of the house! It's our teacher's house.' They stood for another two minutes, motionless, Susanna's heart beating inside her head. Ediye gently squeezed her mum's hand; it was time. She knocked, wanting someone to open the door so desperately. Would whoever it was let them take a peek inside? A woman opened the gate, a Crimean Tatar woman called Arife, a teacher who taught Russian language in the village school. She smiled and invited them into the house.

Two of the rooms were old, the originals, built by Susanna's great-grandfather, but much of the house had been rebuilt and the roof terrace was gone. The back room was the coolest, its wall abutting the side of the mountain itself, and the house did still look as though it was part of the landscape. It ended where the forest began. In the centre of the yard, there was an ancient walnut tree and on top of it lived a red squirrel. The squirrel must have been busy feeding her young, as the base of the tree was piled high with walnut husks. Ediye whispered, 'Mum, it feels like a fairytale.'

'This walnut must have been planted by your great-great-grandfather, like the fig tree,' said Arife. They sat in the garden, under the tree, and their host offered them some fig jam, thick and sweet like honey. Susanna was relieved that a Qırımlı woman lived in the house. Arife had been given the property through TIKA, a Turkish programme that helped Crimean Tatars returning from exile with housing.

Right underneath the windows, on the north side, the brook whispered. Susanna knew that Amza, as a little boy, used to fall asleep to the changing rhythms of this brook, which served as a lullaby in the evenings and as the gentlest of alarm clocks in the mornings. Now, though, Arife complained that the water had become dirty. Up on the mountain the river was blocked, choked, stifled. It struggled to get out and find its original paths, the handmade century-old canals. Only when big rains came did the river push through with force, unclogging itself.

Susanna spotted a curious-looking structure to the left of the house, a remnant of an ancient Qırımlı system of gentle water use. Big boulders were cleverly fitted on top of each other, like drystone walls in the

British countryside, perfectly slotted in together to last for eternity. The boulders went up the mountainside and, on the very top, they held a plank which served as a conductor for water passage. Mountain water trickled down in little rivulets, communicating with each stone until they joined up together into one stream which was used to water the garden. Susanna was surprised about this particular structure, even though she was aware of the history of water use by Crimean Tatars. Like the Ukrainians – for whom the pich, the masonry oven, was sacred, and often anthropomorphised – water was sacred for Qırımlı.

Deep wells and ornate fountains graced every village and town, cared for by everyone and available to all. The private wells were decorated with expensive wood, but instead of wooden buckets, they used small sacks made from sheepskin or thick wool with two sticks at their necks to stop the bags closing. Elderly, often wealthy, 'retired' Tatars took care of the maintenance of the many small canals and walking paths in the forests. When people died, they often left money for the community specifically to keep taking care of the water supply.

I snap back from my reveries. I want to tell Mum Susanna's story, but I do not dare, it is too raw and early now; she does not want to imagine children or grandchildren travelling back to find her stolen home. Susanna was so calm about this other woman living in her ancestral home. But it made me think. What would a return look like for us? Will my parents live to see that day? Will Kakhovka be fought for furiously in the near future? Will the town be razed like all the others in the 20-kilometre radius around it? Will the house, and the summer kitchen where we used to sleep every August, be reduced to rubble? Will the orchard – the place where my elder son nibbled all the low-hanging apples one year, where I ate green walnuts with my younger son – survive? The vegetable garden with its five types of basil? Would the trees feel the punch of the falling missiles, will the underground networks be severed, will the birds, frogs and insects that lived around Dad's huge pond – with its cement menagerie – be permanently disorientated? Or will the place survive, with our family's own personal Russian invaders continuing to live there?

Will Mum want to go back? Is the house irrevocably tainted now by its squatting occupiers, by the pain they caused, by what they got up to? Will someone else live there long enough that we will not have the right to demand it back? If I can ever return, would I need to face those people, or their children, or someone else still, who had made it their home? Or will the Russians retreat and mine everything so heavily that it prevents Kakhovka from being habitable again for many years to come? If so, will the plants take over, will the birds come back, would a thousand frogs – too light to set off the mines – overcrowd Dad's pond?

I feel a ruddy shade of panic crawl up the veins of my chest and into my cheeks. Susanna's story may very well be my future. Or my children's. I am scared that this will be me, as a much older woman, coming back to a place which (even if it is returned to Ukraine) will no longer belong to my family. The history that we managed to sprout, plant and root in, all plucked out and thrown in the bin. What about Liusia and Viktor's graves? Will they still be there at all? Or will the tombstones have been requisitioned to construct some dreadful bridge or ugly fortification?

In occupied areas of Ukraine today, Russian invaders aim to erase local history in order to inject their own. Town names, and the street names within them, are being changed. Mass graves are cemented over, Potyomkin villages — impressive on the surface but all for show — erected above them. I recently watched a video, intended to impress a Russian audience and (presumably) intimidate Ukrainian viewers. It was of a man, a high-ranking Russian soldier now in Mariupol, saying, without looking at the camera, 'Speak Russian or die.'

Dad drove back to Ukraine, to Voznesensk, to his sister, in early September 2022, in the aftermath of a colossal fight with Mum. Besides, he couldn't function in Europe, he said. For all his talk of Europeanising and modernity, it was the European idea of Ukraine that Dad loved and wanted to exist in. Europe itself meant nothing to him. And he did not want to be unemployed and to exist on benefits. He needed a purpose, and even though there might be many opportunities for displaced young Ukrainians who spoke multiple languages, or had energy to learn and strive, there was nothing for my father's generation. Or, at least, there was nothing for my dad. Despite their fight, and the icy silence that wedged itself between them, Dad did ask Mum if she would go back with him. She said no. She could not see herself living in Ukraine but not living in her own home. She stayed behind.

'If by 2027 we still cannot return home,' she told me, 'I will join Dad. Maybe we can buy a little khalupka [a dingy little rundown house] in a village by the Buh River, perhaps there might be trees growing there already, and I can plant my tomatoes. I want to die in Ukraine. But I want to live first.'

I am asked to cook for and talk at a fundraiser for Ukraine, to which a hundred people are coming to eat, listen and donate. The theme of the evening is 'The Meaning of Home'. I make fifty jars of fermented pickles, then huge vats filled with carefully prepared magenta borsch. I make bread which is sweet, salty and sour; I make pudding that tastes like the end of a good evening. This is the easy part.

I don't find public speaking difficult, at least not when it's about Ukraine or my family, as it's what I know. The words normally just fall out of me, one after the other, all pushed out by the tightness of love in my chest, with my brain doing almost no work. But when I start thinking about this particular speech, the theme of the evening – the meaning of home – I am suddenly dumbstruck.

How can I translate the English word 'home' into Ukrainian? The etymology of the English 'home' means residency, but over time – and presumably with the development of abstract thought and concept – the meaning of the word became intangible. A home no longer has to literally be a house: there is space for the esoteric idea of a 'home'. It is not so in Ukrainian, which is why I am stuck. The word dodomu in Ukrainian is an adverb meaning 'to go home'. But there is no word for 'home' in the same way that there is in English. Dim, pronounced deem, is the literal building, the house and the home.

I have never thought about why we do not have a more intangible word for the concept of home in Ukrainian before today. I message my closest friend, Caroline, who is from Shropshire. It is late evening and she is on the way to a gig, but she replies immediately and passionately. She says, 'Only a country and a people who are all about home don't have a word for it. Because the meaning of home is so much more than a word to Ukraine. It's innate. Because Ukrainians are born with an understanding of it before they even know it. It's the reason why the country was united in a moment when the invasion began. Because it's a reflex.'

I send the same question to my cousin Ira, but her answer is different. She says, 'Olia, it's because we have been moved around so much, unable to settle somewhere, unable to pass anything on, no heirlooms, no houses, in many cases very little history. How much history, the names, the toponyms, the records, have been destroyed by Russia? We didn't have time to sit down and develop a word for "home". If you have a house, you cling to it and don't mess around. The physical and emotional and abstract is one.'

So perhaps, I think, our word for 'dim' or 'khata', to us, always sounds like home. It describes, most importantly, the emotional abode: the intangible comes first; the physical building does not require a separate word or concept.

Liuda Mardarenko, floodplains by Lyubymivka village, Kherson region, 2014

8

The World Before the Dam

In September 2022, six months into the war and five months after my parents' escape from Kakhovka, Putin announces that my native region of Kherson is now part of Russia. It doesn't feel real, at all. What does feel real is to sit on the floor by the kitchen door, to pick up a brush and some house paint and start painting it.

My kitchen door is made from rough plywood, with not much texture. I dab the entire surface in pale pink, using a dry sea sponge. Once it's just dry, I pick up a Ukrainian cat-hair brush and start making marks with egg-yolk yellow. First, a flower in the centre of the door. I want it to be a sunflower, but it looks more like a huge daffodil. Then, with racing green, I paint some lines for stems. More flowers. Then I dip my finger in some chalk paint, a Rodmell purple with a speck of white, pressing it in slowly until symmetrical grape clusters appear.

I listen to a Ukrainian news podcast on my phone while I work. It tells me I can never return home again. I continue painting symbols of the South, things that are found in every house and every field of my home region. I believe that if I conjure them up, if I spend time making them present here in my kitchen thousands of kilometres away, they cannot disappear. These symbols will suck in all the bad news that's coming out of my phone, which will tumble and churn in an invisible turbine until the information vanishes forever, proving that what is happening in Kherson is not true and not real.

I paint two birds perching on the grapevine, and two spiders climbing up it, for luck. The sunflower-daffodil-grapevine plant is starting to resemble a tree of life. I paint a small blue pond with two fish at the bottom. Then I go over the whole door with my brush, adding more swirls of circular energy. I dip the wispy soft brush in paint, put its tip on the door first, then gently push down, creating a tear-shaped mark repeating itself all around the grapes, the flowers and the critters.

THE WORLD BEFORE THE DAM

I am not trained in painting, but that never stopped me. The year the war started, there was a sudden, head-spinning outburst of information about Ukrainian culture online. I learned so much, and was inspired. I would glimpse the rich ochres and blues of Ukrainian peasant wall ornaments in old books, I would ride on the backs of Mariya Prymachenko's famous beasts, and bury my body into plump faded peonies by Kateryna Bilokur, then I would pick up a brush and have a go at healing my pain. One of the biggest discoveries for me was Polina Rayko, a woman local to my area, an autodidact, a self-healer.

Rayko was born in the Oleshky village, near the Oleshky Sands, one of the biggest deserts in Europe. It lies just to the left of Kakhovka, about an hour's drive away from the New Kakhovka Dam. Her small house stood right near the shore of the Dnipro River, by the plavni. Before the 1950s, the Dnipro, a huge, thick river splitting Ukraine into two parts – the left bank and the right bank – still looked its best natural self. Throughout the windy, dusty steppe, by the river banks, lived pockets of oasis. The river's bends were punctuated by an ecological phenomenon that we call plavni: floodplains. Plavni have a very important place in the South Ukrainian psyche; they are as ancient as the history of the Black Sea and they appeared at roughly the same time, after the glaciers melted.

Accounts of how the place used to look, recorded by both Eastern and Western European travellers from the eighteenth and nineteenth centuries, are fascinating.

The picture they paint is familiar; some of the plavni did survive and I recognise the descriptions. In August 2018, my husband Joe and I took kayaks to a plavni area called Krynky, a narrow stretch of water, thick with waterlilies and surrounded by a jungle of willows. Bullrush was queen of the floodplains, powerful and tall with a brown porous head. In her shade, arrowheads poked their wedge-shaped leaves out of the water, and bur-reeds bore flail-like clusters. The floating ferns, the river's natural filters, looked like butterfly wings, as if alive and fluttering across the water. Rosettes of water chestnuts would explode here and there like fireworks. Endless clusters of heart-shaped waterlilies, white and yellow, were dotted tightly along the river. They clutched at our oars with their mermaid-fingered roots; it was so hard to push the kayaks through them that the effort caused our fingers to blister. The seeds of the yellow waterlilies would float when ripe, resembling frog spawn, then sink all the way to the riverbed like a thousand stars. Stars so hardy, so eternal that they'd germinate even in the depths of half-frozen, March-time silt.

In the distant past, the forest near the floodplains served as home to a menagerie: foxes and wolves, badgers, wild goats and boars, small wildcats, even bears and elks. Within the plavni nested the birds. There used to be so many: wild geese and spoonbills, swans and ducks, great and little bustards, cranes and egrets, Dalmatian pelicans, black grouse and pheasants, storks, wild pigeons, corncrakes, moorhens, steppe eagles, hawks and gulls.

The sloping white shores of soft clay were an integral part of people's livelihoods, too. Here, people planted fruit trees, stored wood, fished and grew vegetables.

It was living within the plavni that inspired Rayko's images. She worked within them, singing as she worked, and she would paint at night, depicting what she saw around her during the day. Her story is both ordinary and extraordinary, as devastating as it is beautiful. She had a hard life. She grew up in poverty and worked hard her whole life in collectivised Soviet farming, planting wind-blocking strips of trees along the steppe. When the Soviet Union collapsed, she made a little money by selling the vegetables she grew at the market. She married a man and they had two children. Then suddenly, in early 1994, her daughter died in a car crash, then her husband died a year later. Her son became an alcoholic. He raided her house, stole her money and, eventually, went to prison. It was only when he was in prison that Rayko finally had a moment to breathe, or to grieve.

One day in 1998, she decided to spruce up her fence and painted it. Her neighbour admired her work, saying, 'Polina, why don't you also paint two peace doves on the fence?' She exclaimed that she couldn't paint like an artist, but that she would think about it. She did eventually paint the doves... and then she couldn't stop painting. She couldn't believe what was emerging from under her rough, painter-decorator brush. She painted her gate, then the inside walls of her house. Her paintings were eventually to cover every centimetre of her home, including the walls and ceilings. The first room that she painted is dark; the colours are dark and so are the themes. There is a black raven, with a toothy beak. He carries a white baby-bird in his mouth and underneath sits the bird-mother, crying.

As you move through the house, the rooms become lighter and more colourful. In one room, there are depictions of angels. One of them shows Rayko herself, holding a basket of flowers; above her, a pair of cherubs whisk away towards the sky, holding a rocket. There is Jesus and the Virgin Mary. There are her three dead sisters, bearing angel wings, perching on three crescents, surrounded by doves and flowers. There is a monastery. All these images are drawn over a background of celestial blue, with flowers — daffodils, sunflowers, daisies — like stars scattered around and between the angels.

After her son's death, Rayko painted the room where he used to live. It is her plavni room. The murals on the walls depict water and bulrushes, beaked fish and turtles, storks and cranes and boats. In one of them sits her bearded husband; he looks like a domovyk, a Ukrainian imp-like house spirit. Her husband loved to fish, so from his boat stretches a fishing rod. He is playing a lute and he is accompanied by a row of bottles, some filled with red and white wine and some with moonshine.

In the past, when I returned to Ukraine from the UK, at least twice a year, I would fly into Kyiv and then take a rickety sleeper train to Kherson, my home region's main city, roughly the size of Birmingham. It was a twelve-hour journey. Ukraine is huge, so much bigger than people realise. 'It is even bigger than France!' I used to say proudly. As if its size made it more interesting or significant than people believed.

The train's rhythmic beat, tu-dum tu-dum, tu-dum, would bounce off dark-green forests and drown in creeks and valleys until we reached the stark flatness of the steppe, and my stop. Kherson train station. I would arrive in the morning, shoulders and hips sore from the stiffness of the train's bunk bed, teeth unbrushed, heart beating slightly faster. Soon I will be with Mum and Dad, my brother, my extended family and pets, the vine arbour and the orchard, the garden and Mum's cooking. She'd always know what I wanted to eat; it would never change, but she would still ask me the night before every time.

'What shall I cook for your arrival?' A sweet checking in, a ritual we had that reassured me I was coming home. I would laugh and say, 'You know what I want!' The answer was always dumplings, with syr, a fresh cheese similar to quark, and I would hasten to remind her to make sure to slightly over-season the filling, otherwise the balance with the thick sweet-tasting sour cream and butter would be a little off, and I would only eat ten dumplings instead of thirty. I couldn't wait to gorge myself, to feel so full of dumplings and my mum's love that I would need to have a lie-down.

In Kakhovka, Mum would be putting a huge pot of salted water on to boil, while my dad would already be waiting for me on the platform in Kherson station. His heart-breaking, crooked gait so easily spotted in the crowd, his eyes creased and smiling, a neat, freshly trimmed beard and haircut. Then we would drive for an hour, catching up on his work and my studies, or his work and my work, his new diet fad, my friends, politics. Whatever the circumstances, I would always ask, 'Sho v Ukrayini?' ('How is Ukraine?') On the way, in the warmer months, I'd glimpse the fields – the colour of the sun above them – stretching across the wide, but no longer wild, steppe.

Ukraine's flag suddenly made total sense: here it was, the yin and yang, the dark, warm and fertile feminine earth and icy-bright masculine skies. In the past 200 years, the deep-rooted sea of kovyl (wild feather grass) had been churned up; turned into a sea of shallow-rooted crops. The sky is still the same, though, so vast that you feel as though you might see other galaxies in the distance, even in daylight. In Ukrainian, the Milky Way is called Chumatskiy Shlyah: 'the path of the Chumaks'. Chumaks were medieval traders who carried salt and other goods, in huge wagons dragged by oxen, across the steppes from Crimea. Their journey was punctuated by stars.

From the car, I glimpse numerous canals, narrow and ugly, lined with concrete. They are capillaries coming from the reservoir artery, which used to be a river. Closer to home, we pass the thick vein of the North Crimean Canal.

Even though it is wheat, corn and sunflower fields that dominate now, there are still small, virgin patches of unploughed land, plants that have been left undisturbed — apart from the hooves of nomads' horses — for thousands of years. There are remnants of the Scythian babas of proto-Iranic tribes: prehistoric monuments perched on manmade mounds, ancient burial grounds pregnant with bones and the unknown. And despite having been worked for two centuries now, you can still feel that energy. The landscape is thick with history, mystical, magnetic, sometimes scary. The black soil saturated in equal measure with death and life, two sides of the same coin.

In Ukraine, they call the steppe an upside-down forest. There may be not much showing above ground, even if the grass is tall, but underneath lies a massive system of roots and bulbs. The black soil, chornozem, was so fertile it was rumoured that the Germans took tonnes of it home in trucks after retreating in 1943. It is widely known that Ukraine's black soil has been sold on the black market since 1992.

The steppe stretches from Mongolia through Central Asia and all through Ukraine, finishing by Central Europe. If you look at it from space, it looks like a subcutaneous fat deposit on Eurasia's belly. Ancient and modern movements of people, produce, cultures and languages were possible because of this flat stretch of grassland. It is also one of the reasons why the territory of modern Ukraine has always been so vulnerable: there are protective mountains in the west, but the border is bare and unprotected in the east.

Out of my immediate family, my brother and I are the only two who were born in the Kherson region. Both Mum and Dad were born in Voznesensk, two and a half hours north in the neighbouring region of Mykolayiv. Mum's brother Slava, however, married a Kakhovka local, Lyudmyla Fedorchuk. Aunt Liuda is not my blood relative, but in this case, water is thicker than blood. The water is that of the floodplains of our birthplace, teeming with life: tadpoles, insects, waterlilies, fish, birds and the tips of languid weeping willow branches.

When I started writing about food, it was my Uncle Slava's wife Liuda, a third-generation Kakhovchanka, who I ran to when I wanted to learn about local dishes or local history. I was fascinated by the names of dishes she taught me: tuzluk (lamb broth cooked over fire), pekmez (molasses made from watermelon juice), liok (herbs crushed with garlic and salt and tempered by hot liquid to make a sauce). These sonorous names contained so much within them. Before Catherine the Great annexed the Crimean Khanate mainland territories in 1774, the lands I was born into were pretty wild. The steppe was a sea of deep-rooted grasses and fertile floodplains, but had very few sources of water. I often imagine the giant yellow steppe as a reflection of the sun itself, a star reflected in a star, heat squared. Both stars ravenous. Water, hungrily, absorbed by one, then evaporated by the other. Though inhabited by pockets of Cossack settlements and nomadic tribes such as

Nohay Tatars, it was mostly empty and unspoiled, so the potential of the land was clear. Given just that extra bit of water and a bunch of talented farmers, it could become a cornucopia.

One of the first things Catherine did was to banish the Nohays who pastured their herds along the Dnipro. These pastoral nomadic tribes never settled, moving along with their herds in family groups called otars in the summer, or bigger groups called auls in winter. Otays, their shelters on wheels, were wrapped in felt; the coals burning inside on a special stove puffed smoke out of a chimney and into the whistling winds of the open steppe. These tribes were pushed out into the territories of modern Romania and Turkey, plans to replace them with Russian settlers — sent to make the steppe agriculturally viable — already in the works. Catherine called this new province Taurida.

The first wave of colonisation was by Russian and Ukrainian nobility, invited in by the Russian Empire. But they needed specialists to develop the area and the wealthy resettled landlords had no interest in that. So Alexander I started a campaign to attract foreign colonists, especially Germans and Mennonite farmers from West Prussia, to move in and help. (This is how hundreds of German villages and Lutheran churches ended up scattered all over the grasslands.)

For the first three-quarters of my life, I thought that I had grown up in a forgotten, unimportant place. Kakhovka:

such an awkward word for a foreigner to pronounce. And who cared anyway, when there was Paris and London, Beijing, Washington and all the other places that mattered? What I did not understand at the time was that Ukraine – but also specifically Kakhovka and its surrounding area – has always been important strategically. When the USSR built a hydropower station and the North Crimean Canal in the 1950s and 1960s, to supply Crimea with water, it immediately added an extra level of geopolitical importance to my birthplace. Crimean Tatars had once carefully managed their water supply, so there was enough for the needs of their land and their people. Now, with Crimean Tatars forcibly scattered from their homeland, the water supply was faltering.

Before we get to the bad bits, I want to say that I feel lucky to know about the ghost of the steppe floodplains. My aunt Liuda, as a small child, caught the last glimpses of the true Dnipro River and its unique shores in the Kherson region, as well as the gentle local agrarian culture which was soon to be vanished forever. Aunt Liuda loves talking of the world 'before the dam'. When she describes Khersonshyna back then, she says, 'That kovyl grass, swaying, a whole sea of it! The land was like a mirror, tsilyna [whole or virgin land], never ploughed and stretching as far as the eye can see, to the edge of the Earth.' Around Kakhovka and the rest of the Ukrainian South, there was a strong tradition of working in tandem with nature. When grey snows thawed in March, there were periods when the water level on the Dnipro River was very high, peaking at the end of April and early May. This resulted in the plains being naturally flooded, hence the name, plavni: the floodplains.

'Aunt Liuda, I don't understand. So if the floodplains flooded the area naturally, how did people deal with it?' Liuda's voice sounds like a thousand bells are ringing. 'Olechka, ty znayesh...!' ('Olia, do you know...!') She herself mixes Ukrainian and Russian, the dialect we call surzhyk. She continues, at a thousand miles per hour. 'Before the dam, it was so different! First of all everyone spoke Ukrainian here in Kakhovka. There was none of this surzhyk. I even remember the words we used then, I remember it being normal, Ukrainian words for things, local Ukrainian words to describe what was around us.' (The Russification which would trample the Ukrainian language did not take hold until the 1960s and 1970s.)

'Aunt Liuda, OK I know, but the floodplains!' 'The plavni, yes!' Her voice becomes nonchalant, regulated, as she talks about something that used to be mundane. 'The water flooded, but predictably and almost always at the same time as the snow melted. So people knew where to build and where not to build, where the areas will not be flooded and will soon turn into a meadow. Rozumiyesh?' ('Understand?') I understand. During the natural flooding, any slightly elevated areas turned into islets, where weeping willows grew. They did not build on areas that would normally be flooded. People knew where these islands would pop up, with their fertile soil and healthy meadows, so they were used as pasture grounds.

Liuda raises her finger, and closes her eyes, then pauses for a few beats more with her eyes closed, in a kind of suspended, slow-motion blink. She is in oracle mode. It is no longer her speaking, it is the past, and the past always comes as an oracle. 'Ooooolechka! Those boats! Ploskodonka [a flat-bottomed boat]! The base of the boat was flat and large enough…'

Dramatic pause.

'… For a cow to be safely transported to a little island. The cow would be dropped off there, you know, to pasture!' 'Just left alone there on this island?' 'Well yeah! What does the cow care? The boat is big and, on the island, it's grass and flowers everywhere. Then, of course, the owner would row back to land, but would return three times a day to milk the cow, maybe give extra feed. Some people even used these islands as allotments. Even aubergines were still not common, you know, but some people started cultivating them on the islands. They grew so well under the hot sun. And then they came to build…' Her voice now thunders and mocks, 'Anooooother Great Construction Project of Kommunizm.'

This world of Homeric flat boats and pasture islands was not compatible with the bright future of post-war socialism, with its accent on factories and big industries. Liuda's story is short and personal. 'O-lech-ka. We knew this family, knew someone from a small village near Kakhovka, you know near the village, Mala

Kakhovka? Soviet officials showed up at their house and announced that they had three days... THREE DAYS, Olichkaaaaa, to pack their things and leave. Three. Days. The bulldozers were coming.'

Liuda's personal account is borne out in *Poem about the Sea*, a 1956 Soviet film written by legendary Ukrainian director Oleksandr Dovzhenko. After Stalin's death and Beria's execution, Khrushchev was keen to throw dirt on Stalin's projects and to show his benevolence (albeit briefly), so there was scope to make critical films such as this. The film depicted the construction of the Kakhovka Dam. In one scene, the main protagonist visits a family, the man grumbling, pulling out wood pillars from his clay cottage before the bulldozers run over the skeleton of the house. In the next, another homeowner takes the last frame from his house's window, then pauses and turns his head to the side, covers his eyes and waves for the bulldozers to go ahead. In the most heartbreaking vignette, an older woman presses her cheek to the inside wall of her clay khata. She sings mournfully to her house, 'How is it that I leave you, my darling?' as if the house is the mother and she the daughter who must go and leave her behind, never to return.

At the end, the narrator says, 'The great Zaporizhzhia Meadow sunk under the Dnipro water, and the old crosses on the grandfathers' tombs sank for eternity. All the beauty our parents and grandparents knew in their childhood disappeared forever.'

The New Kakhovka hydropower plant (HPP) and dam was one of the last projects launched under Stalin's so-called Great Plan of Transformation of Nature. The end goal was to create an irrigation system which could support up to 1.5 million hectares of land for farming, as well as watering more than 1.7 million hectares on the territory of Southern Ukraine and Northern Crimea, which, before, were not suitable for farming. As part of this initiative, the 550-kilometre-long Southern-Ukrainian Channel was planned, stretching from Zaporizhzhia through Askania Nova and Sivash to its final end in Kerch, Crimea. The Soviet authorities' goal to maximise agricultural potential paid scant regard to the sacrifices that would be needed for this. Up to 2,800 hectares of already existing and fertile arable land were flooded, up to 31,000 people were forcibly displaced from their homes, about a hundred villages located along the original banks of the Dnipro were flooded. Along with the villages, cultural heritage was destroyed; Scythian and Cossack burial places and churches in Velyky Luh ('The Great Floodplains Forest') floodplains between Kakhovka and Zaporizhzhia perished. Existing infrastructure, such as the mines of Krivbass, was damaged because of water leaks and pressure.

The plavni on the Dnipro shores in the Lepetykha, Kairov and Oleshky localities were an integral part of people's livelihoods, where inhabitants such as Polina Rayko planted fruit trees, grew vegetables and fished. The sloping shores were made out of soft clay, just like the place five or ten minutes' walk from my childhood home where I loved playing with my cousin Aliona, which I romantically christened 'the dunes'. Some of the shores in Kakhovka were fortified by granite in the 1970s, but initially a lot of these natural soft slopes were left as they were, so when the extra water came, the shores collapsed, along with the livelihoods they had supported. The people removed from their homesteads, land and way of life were transferred to Soviet high-rises; many of them were put to work on the new rice and cotton fields and cotton-processing plants.

The floods caused irreversible changes in natural conditions, damaging for fish and birds that used to settle along the banks of the old Dnipro. Animals and plant life perished, because they couldn't adapt to the new conditions. The river water itself, once considered clean, was no longer suited for human consumption because of aggressive algae blooming, which further damaged the ecological situation. In order to make things work, the Soviets decided to construct another two dams above the Kakhovka HPP, killing the original Dnipro River by turning it into a cascade of gigantic ponds.

The building work itself was a shambles. Despite finishing a year ahead of plan, the conditions for construction workers were dire. Thousands of people had flocked to the site from all over Ukraine and the Soviet Union in search of work. But there was no accommodation and working hours were from 9 a.m. to midnight. The archives reveal letters that say 'there is no water', 'there is no bread', 'there is no sewer', 'there is no money'. The 160 houses that were built in the emerging town of New Kakhovka had no plumbing, as there were pipe shortages. The fierce steppe winds carrying sand were so strong that it was impossible to work without goggles. The only thing in the shops was barley flour, and you had to queue for that for hours. People who came to demand their wages were turned away and told to work harder.

In the end, the Soviet goals were not achieved. Even such a gargantuan water storage facility as the Kakhovka Reservoir was not enough to provide water for 1.5 million hectares of land, only for 400,000 hectares. They had miscalculated. Besides, because the Soviets were artificially drying marshes in the northern parts of Ukraine to make more space for arable land, not enough water flowed down to fill the reservoir.

This is why the Dnipro River of my childhood was so stagnant, reeking of green slimy algae, like a sponge in a dirty sink. Later, the industrial waste, such as radionuclides from the Zaporizhzhia nuclear plant, oil deposits and industrial waste, was flushed into the reservoir, turning its silt deposits into poison.

The Soviets may not have achieved their objectives with the completion of the dams, but there was nevertheless a hideous silver lining for them. During the Second World War, German forces succeeded in building a pontoon bridge across the Dnipro River, giving them access to Crimea without any significant resistance from the Soviet Army. But thanks to the reservoir, in future Crimea would be off limits. If there was another invasion, the Soviets could blow up the dams, creating a quagmire that would take at least a month to dry.

The image of the new town, the Soviet New Kakhovka and its hydropower plant (New Kakhovka HPP), is so deeply embedded in my whole being that, in my head, I can see it from all angles. From above, the view of a cormorant flying by. From below, a pike chasing bait dragged by a speedboat. From the changing shapes and colours of car windows: a Lada window with floral curtains in the 1980s, Mum's first baby-blue Volkswagen in the 2000s, the tinted windows of Dad's Audi in the early 2020s.

Every time we left my Old Kakhovka hometown, or came back to it, we would pass the New Kakhovka HPP and the dam. I took pleasure in driving over the bridge, alongside the dam. Our car, like a tiny cat, rubbing against the shins of a giant. I loved looking out and watching the huge swathes of water all the way below, dotted with tufts of green islets. The realisation of how high we were, and that to the side of us tonnes and tonnes of water were held by concrete, was exhilarating. The dam always felt like the promise of home. New Kakhovka HPP is about 16 kilometres away from my parents' house. Passing it meant that I was twenty minutes away from hugging my mum.

In terms of the endless waters, as a kid I always thought to just call it Dnipro, but the adults would often correct me and say the word 'reservoir'. I remember taking this on board, but I didn't really understand the difference. But in 2014, when Crimea was annexed, the plant, the dam and the canal shapeshifted in my head from innocent childhood landmarks to objects that signified extreme danger.

I'd already written the words above when, on 6 June 2023, I woke up to terrible news. The dam, controlled by the Russians from the beginning of the full-scale invasion, had been blown up. New Kakhovka was flooded. For the next few days, I watch an apocalypse unfold. A mother and child on the roof of their house in Oleshky, surrounded by the murky waters. People trying to save dogs in flooded Kherson, or cattle and deer in rural areas. Most of the floodplain forests, islands and meadows that survived the construction of the dam in the 1950s were now destroyed. More videos online: people clutching the endangered birch mice, the endemic sand voles and the thick-tailed three-toed jerboas from the Falz-Fein nature reserve. They reckon at least half the population of these critters was wiped out by the flood. The river was the nesting point for herons, coots, mute swans and glossy ibises, their newly hatched chicks washed with the toxins and mines into the Black Sea. Around 50,000 Black Sea dolphins had already been terribly affected by Russian sonars; now, the mines swept from Kakhovka and Kherson exploded on impact, causing them further physical and acoustic injuries.

THE WORLD BEFORE THE DAM

I look at videos from New Kakhovka. In the town's centre, the municipal building is covered in water up to its chin. I read the caption: 'Typhoid and swans, all in one place.' I watch a sea of fish flapping their sun-slicked silver bodies on silted ground. Beneath, it says, 'Due to the draining of the Kakhovka Reservoir, local aquatic and floodplain plants are likely to disappear, and the dried-out area will be filled with dangerous weeds.' More images of sorrow: Odesa shores receive the debris: a sofa, a wardrobe, someone's entire red roof. A dog arrives, alive, clinging to a piece of plank; so does a doe.

While the flood was an ecological disaster, there was so much else lost to the waters. A month later, I see images of Rayko's house museum. More than half the murals are gone, the magic plavni beasts eaten by the flood and the angels drowned. Like the ancient burial sites and the churches lost to the dam's construction, the Ukrainian culture that was rebuilt afterwards had now, in turn, been destroyed. What will we be left with? More soulless Soviet buildings? That day I pick up a picture frame in my London home, the one of my brother and me in a dusty field, and I paint two gold-crested cranes on each side, along with markings similar to Rayko's. I promise her that I will not forget.

I finished decorating my kitchen door within a month, but I could not stop painting, and kept adding little details on to it for the following year. Whenever bad things happened, I was there, adding strokes in gouache or tempera, throwing it into a compositional misbalance. It was over-embellished, matching the ebbs and flows of my anxiety. But staring at it brought me joy and moments of quiet reflection. In the end, from its centre, a flowering fern grew. The old Ukrainian legend goes: she who finds the flowering fern will be able to understand and communicate with animals. At its lowest branches, two owls sit, one slightly startled and funny-looking (that's me) and one that looks more composed (my husband Joe). The two spiders climbing upwards towards good luck are our children, singing birds guard the tree and grapevines that cling to it. I keep threatening to paint over it, to start afresh, paint something better, but Joe won't let me.

Rayko's paintings were not forgotten, and I doubt they will be any time soon. Foreign press reported the loss of her art – a pretty big deal – and in Ukraine her works were reproduced on silk scarves, her sister angels embroidered on Etnodim blouses. It wasn't just the paintings, it was her story that was the most important, the channelling of grief into colourful, healing patterns. In all this pain and destruction, I hope that nature will be allowed to heal itself with no obstruction. Let river shores turn into infant forests. I also hope that, like Rayko, we remember not to hate forever, but to create through grief, to record stories, to paint gardens with paint and brush, and with seeds, soil and water.

With Wilfred, Auvergne, France 2024

Epilogue

A Summit in France

France, August 2024, diary entries

It is high August, and I am trying to fall asleep. I am lying on my favourite swampy-green sheets, crumpled linen, both textured and soft. A plump pillow is sandwiched between my thighs: a hip-steadying habit from when I was pregnant with my sons. The spinning head of a fan is fluttering air across my body. When it pauses for a few seconds at the top of my outstretched hand, I can feel the full heat of this summer. The air is thick with damp heat that clings and burns.

It is high August, and I am trying to fall asleep. I feel curious about what may await me in my sleep, even though it could terrify me. I've suffered from sleep paralysis since my early twenties, but it has intensified so much since the beginning of the full-scale invasion that I am haunted by it every week. The terrors I feel, while being awake with my brain but stuck in my body, have been so horrifying this summer, especially since the Okhmatdyt children's hospital in Kyiv was bombed by Russia, that I ask my GP to refer me for a mental health assessment.

The other night, the whirring sound of this benign, cooling fan transformed into loud, demonic noises blasting at me. I know that I experience an incomplete transition between REM and the conscious state. It's a glitch that whisks those two states into a vision. Hallucinations I have been experiencing have become increasingly audial, always involving loud sounds, and I don't know why. The episode was probably no longer than a few seconds, but it felt like forty minutes. The deafening music roars from the fan and then, as always, the demons appear. This time three round, floating faces. I can't quite see them, they are always a 'presence'. They are speaking tongues, but the timbres of their voices are those of my grandmothers and my aunt. I try to scream, but nothing comes out of my mouth. I realise that, even though I cannot move any part of my body, I can control my breathing. So I take very deep breaths, in-in-in-in and, just when I think I cannot go any further, in once again. Then a very deep exhale. I release myself from my overworked mind and finally fall asleep. Despite these night terrors, I am doing well. The war has forced me to find new ways to take care of myself.

Even before the war, it was said that worrying is the Ukrainian national pastime. We always feel as though

EPILOGUE

trouble is right around the corner. So, when it finally happened in 2022, some experienced the war as almost cathartic. Finally, we could be our best selves: struggling at everyday life, but almost superhuman in times of crisis.

This week, the week of the scorching August air, I am in central France and I have recently turned forty. We are having our first family (and friends) summit in exile. My mum came on a nine-hour coach journey from Milan. My cousin Iryna and her family drove from Berlin. Friends drove and flew from London, Glasgow and Belgium. My brother, sadly, was unable to make it. His regiment was being moved from their base in Kyiv to a much scarier place. My dad was not able to leave Ukraine on his own. His neurological tremors have become too severe and he struggles to walk for longer than ten minutes. Besides, since no flights can come out of Ukraine, the journey is too gruelling even for a young, healthy person. Dad would have needed either to drive for nine hours to Moldova or take a nine-hour train journey to Kyiv, then catch more trains to get to airports in neighbouring countries. This is one of the reasons why the rest of my displaced family is not with us. My internally displaced friend sent me a voice note saying, 'I am worried that they will mobilise my husband while I am away. I cannot leave him. I feel like we are in the Soviet Union again, prisoners inside our own country. They have created another Iron Curtain for some of us who cannot leave or do not want to leave loved ones behind.'

So it is a limited summit, only seven members and four generations of our family are present. This French house is on top of a small mountain and the view from the back terrace looks stunningly like Western Ukraine. Tall, rich greenish-brown pine trees, thick juicy oaks, tall dry frilly bronze grass and a sea of the lacy seed-heads of wild carrots. Wild strawberry plants that bore fruit in June are scattered around the front door and grapevines stretch their leafy hands through the wooden shutters, casting impenetrable shadows over their ripening greenish-mauve fruit. The main festive table is outside. We have actually set up three tables together to make one, just like we did at Liusia's house and just like we did at Mum's in Kakhovka. We have a kazanok pot gently swaying over a big pile of auburn coals. Inside, a Transcarpathian paprika stew bubbles gently, smelling of meaty smoke, spices and very good summer vegetables. We drink cold young wine, made by Joe the previous autumn. It tastes very Ukrainian, Besarabian even.

During the three-day celebration, our conversations vary. When Mum arrives, one of my best friends bursts into tears. They hadn't seen each other since before the war started. It is difficult to avoid the subject of the war. At least no one asks, 'How do you think it will end?' No one knows.

There is a lot of laughter during these three days. The voices of Liusia, Zhenia, Liuda, Vera and so many more members of our family come out through the jumble of our stories. This time the tales are told in Ukrainian, but translated by me into English for my anglophone friends.

Our three days are also filled with art. The tables are covered by a pink grapes oilcloth I bought at Charleston House in Sussex. A lot of these designs were created at the Omega Workshops, the result of intense creativity by the Bloomsbury Group in spite of the trauma and upheaval of the First and Second World Wars. It somehow feels hopeful that I know and love these patterns that have survived almost a hundred years. I dream of a future revival of the work of the Olexandra Exter's Verbivka peasant workshops in Kyiv about a decade earlier, where modernist and avant-garde motifs were hand-crafted by female Ukrainian artisans. At our family summit we listen to Ukrainian music; we even sing drunkenly one evening, my mum, cousin Ira and I, wailing a sad song about a falcon and freedom, Liusia's favourite.

The day after the big celebration, my cousin proposes we use the large table to teach the children how to make a mosaic. She has been practising this, as well as a myriad of other art therapy techniques, in Berlin, helping displaced Ukrainian adults and children to rebuild neurone connections and to heal themselves. We use special pliers to chip off small pieces of glass and ceramics, then stick them on a mosaic, gently, where it feels good to do so. The children are using pre-made patterns of birds and artichoke flowers and I am gluing my pieces freestyle, clumsily but enjoyably, on a tatty wooden tray. Of course I attempt to depict the Askania gold-crested crane, the same I painted on the frame of the photograph of me and my brother in that dusty field near our childhood home. Ira explains to us what is happening in our brain while we work.

I think: this is it. This is the Ukrainian-ness that is in my blood. This thirst for curiosity, this thirst for creativity, the capacity to allow your brain to find a space to exist in two unavoidable worlds. I voice this to my family and friends. I say: grief is grief, and it is human and universal. Most of us live in a state of war, whether actual or personal. Everyone loses their loved ones, there is rarely anyone who escapes this feeling. But we must find space and snippets of time where grief is allowed to bloom, then an equal amount of time when we allow ourselves to rest and recover. It is important to accept the existence of the dark, but it is our responsibility to hold on to the light.

After everybody leaves, someone sends me a video. A man who still lives in my hometown is walking through a local area where, two years ago, there was water. The sun-kissed water that once flowed past my parents' house is no longer there, instead the place is full of four-metre-tall willow trees, an impenetrable jungle of them. It is once more starting to look like it did before the Soviets built the dam in the 1950s. It feels like a miracle.

Aunt Liuda and her family have moved from a soulless apartment block to a little house and they send me a photo of a deeply tanned, shirtless Uncle Slava with a tattoo on his left arm. He sits in front of a huge basin of pears. He is wrapping these pears in newspaper. No suitcase for storing them this time; instead some crates await the primrose-yellow fruit for ripening.

Of course, life is not rosy. The war continues and some people might never recover from their devastating losses. Ira still works as a volunteer psychologist with people from Mariupol. There are whole families who have experienced events so unimaginable that Ira describes their state of mind as if a demon, a darkness, has descended on them and swallowed them whole. My mum's sister Valentina is still living in occupation, looking after her ill daughter, my cousin Svetlana. The Russians still live in my parents' house. We still don't know what will happen, and I know that my night terrors will not leave me any time soon.

But now I know that we are not victims. And we are not just survivors. We, Ukrainians of many ethnicities, cultures and histories, are united. We are scrambling to piece the mosaics of our personal and common history together, to add our family stitches to Ukraine's embroidery, comparing notes and becoming stronger. This story is continuing, but it is time to try and close the circle, to remember the roots, the waterways and floodplains, the black soil. And here I am, living and breathing, writing these words for you, dear reader, to feel and understand our story.

When I finished this book I shared it with Mum and she shared Liusia's wise words about how to nurture rose bushes. She said, 'Olia, always look at the roots. If the roots are strong, it doesn't matter if the wind blows off the pretty petals. If the roots are strong, it doesn't matter if a storm breaks the fragile stem. It will all grow back again.'

Hrebeniuk family tree

- Stepan Mardarenko
  - Olena (m. Vasilii Paskov)
    - Vera Paskova (m. Oleksii Hrebeniuk)
      - Petro Hrebeniuk (m. Olha Mardarenko)
        - Oleksandr Hrebeniuk
        - Olena Zyk
          - Nikita Hrebeniuk
          - Oleksandra Hrebeniuk
          - Danylo Hrebeniuk
        - Joseph Woodhouse

- Stepan Hrebeniuk (m. Anastasiia)
  - Oleksii Hrebeniuk (m. Vera Paskova)

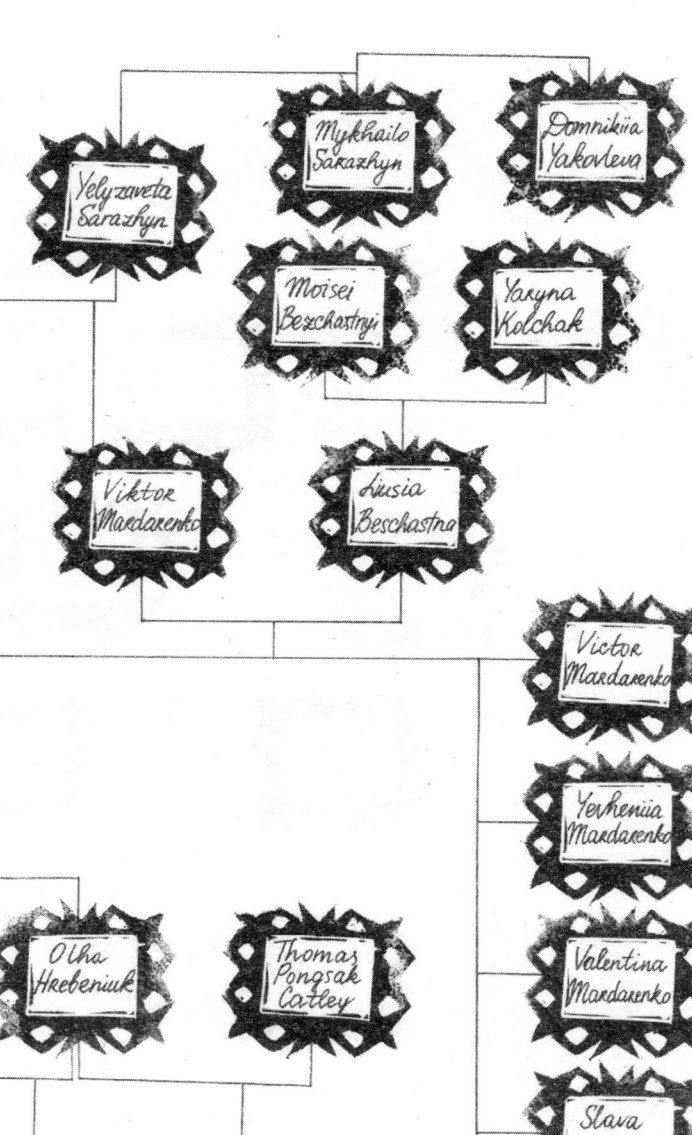

- Yelyzaveta Sarazhyn
- Mykhailo Sarazhyn
- Domnikiia Yakovleva
- Moisei Beschastnyi
- Yaryna Kolchak
- Viktor Mardarenko
- Liusia Beschastna
- Victor Mardarenko
- Yevheniia Mardarenko
- Valentina Mardarenko
- Slava Mardarenko
- Yurii Mardarenko
- Olha Hrebeniuk
- Thomas Pongsak Catley
- Wilfred Woodhouse
- Alexander Catley

Acknowledgements

Usually when people write memoirs they have a bit, or a lot, of distance from the event. Even though I do also write about events that have taken place more than a hundred years ago in this book, what my family went through all those years ago has happened again. Not one generation of my family has escaped dispossession, deportation or war. While I was writing, the war raged on, so it was a particularly difficult process. However, one of the reasons why I was so keen to write this book was to close the cycle of intergenerational trauma. To put it all down on paper, so my children can read it, process it and develop a resistance to what's to come.

The process of writing it was admittedly both cathartic and re-traumatising in equal measure. So I am thankful to everyone who worked with me on this book for understanding this, and for working hard to help me protect my mental health during the process. On this note, also a thank you to Sara, a trauma psychiatrist

ACKNOWLEDGEMENTS

who helped me at the very start of the war and to all NHS mental health professionals that followed after.

This book would not exist without my big family, so a huge thank you to them all for keeping our history alive. Thank you Ira, Aliona and aunt Liuda for giving me so much of your time, I know it has not been easy to talk while living during such difficult times. To my family in Odesa, to my family in exile in Poland, to my family and friends who still live under occupation and wait for us to liberate them. You are in my thoughts and actions every single day.

Mamo, Tato, you have been through so much, you have lost so much, and still you stand strong, finding your own coping mechanisms. Dad, you confirmed it for me, just how important a sense of purpose is to a human. When you wrote to me and said that you must return to Ukraine and do something, because you will otherwise perish from depression in Berlin, I was so scared. But you are doing such amazing, important work, and I can see how it fills you with strength every day. It has been such an important lesson for me.

Mum, my whole worldview, the wonder and love I have for this world, my vision and self-expression would not be possible without the mirror of your own. Also it is through you, Liusia, Zhenia and Vera that I have formed such a strong understanding of female strength. How lucky I am to have had you all as my role models.

My brother Sasha, you did not have to join in the fight, but you did. To help protect us all, people in Ukraine, and also people in Europe. There is not one night when

ACKNOWLEDGEMENTS

I do not think of you going to sleep in cold and uncomfortable barracks while I go to sleep in my safe and cosy bed. Thank you for speaking to me about the past and especially about your experiences at the beginning of the war. I know it has not been easy.

A special thank you to my friend Katrya Seldonenko for telling me your family story and for your friendship. A special thank you to Silvia Razakova and her mother Giulia and especially her aunt Susanna for sharing their precious Qırımlı family history which allowed me to write the Asret chapter. I do not lose hope that we will be able to return to our homes.

Thank you to everyone at Bloomsbury and Knopf for taking on this project and working so hard. Alexis, Ariel, Juliet, Lauren, Ellen, Anna, George in the UK and also Lexy, Sarah and Sara in the US, and many many more from both publishers. Making a book takes a massive village, and I am grateful to you all. Also Cats and Bats for the singing and Veronika Prykhodko for the family tree design.

Thank you to my publishers for connecting me with Anna Vaux, who helped trail through over 120,000 words I'd written and then patiently and gently help me to arrange the writing into the book it has become. You are one of a kind Anna, thank you for your talent and thank you for your friendship.

As always, Ariella Feiner (my agent of ten whole years!), thank you for being encouraging but never pushy, for giving me confidence and having my back at every step of the way. Thank you Amber for all your

ACKNOWLEDGEMENTS

work. And also to my America-based agent Zoe for helping with things across the pond.

Dear Maria Luniw, I couldn't have coped without your support, I truly couldn't. I am so lucky to have an amazing colleague and friend in you. Dyakuyu, with all my heart.

I know they can't hear me, but I must also say thank you to all my ancestors, knowing what they have been through has given me strength and perspective. At my lowest, I would think – if they survived what they did in isolation, Ukrainians and I can survive with the support of the global community.

So thank you to everyone, all over the world who supported, shared information, donated. To those who donated when my brother joined the Territorial Army which allowed me to buy protective gear for him and 105 Ukrainian civilians in his regiment who decided to stay and defend Kyiv. I want you all to know that you helped save lives.

Thank you to my Patreon community – your support and encouragement meant that I could write this book, donate to good causes, and carry on with my activism.

To all the volunteers and organisations that keep supporting Ukraine. Giles Duly of The Legacy of War and his team – you are incredible. Razom for Ukraine in the USA – you go above and beyond, and have been doing it since 2014, I am so proud to be involved in your work.

To Felicity Spector for going to Ukraine, to its most dangerous parts too, almost every other month since the full-scale invasion and for writing *Bread and War*.

And to everyone else who keeps writing books about Ukraine. Olesya Khromeychuk, Viktoria Amelina, Victoria Belim, Maksym Eristavi, Oleksandr Mykhed, Illia Ponomarenko, Yeva Skalietska, Serhii Plokhy, Timothy Snyder and many many more.

Everyone who has found the time to read the book and give it encouraging words: Nigella Lawson, Serhii Plokhy, Louise Kennedy, Caroline Eden, Elisabeth Luard, and many others. I appreciate you all.

To Alissa Timoshkina, who co-founded Cook For Ukraine with me, and who worked so relentlessly, so hard alongside the team on volunteer basis for whole two years. Thank you to the rest of the team, especially Clerkenwell Boy and Leila Yarjani. To the food community in the UK and the world, food writers, restaurants, organisations, publications, individuals for supporting CookForUkraine and other organisations.

To podcasters Sasha Shevchenko of Ne Na Chasi and Sofia Terlez and Mark Livin for their podcast Prostymy Slovamy. Listening to your work obsessively helped me to finally speak Ukrainian, helped me to remain sane throughout the past three years.

My art teacher Valia, and Ukrainian language teacher to my son, Alina, both of you still living in Ukraine by the Russian border, constantly under missile fire, under perpetual threat but refusing to leave, because why would you – it is the home that you love. I am in awe of you, your integrity, your wisdom, talents and work.

To Caroline, Colin, Dot and Reggie. To Ellie and Jimmy. To Dima Deinega and Anna and Maria.

ACKNOWLEDGEMENTS

Nataliya and Kie and the girls. Gabriella and Mashudu. Also Val Voshchevska. You are all family really, thank you for your support during all these years.

There have been so many people, hundreds of people, for whom empathy is a superpower, not a weakness. I am sorry I do not have space to mention you all. But I want you to know that I am so grateful for your humanity and help.

I wish I'd never had to write this book or that this book only talked about the beauty of Ukraine and her people. But it is what it is, so thank you, dear Reader for buying and reading this book. I hope the light within it stays with you.

Finally, my children Sasha and Wilfred, I hope this book and our heritage will make you feel who you are even more clearly and powerfully. To my husband Joe, without you holding our small unit together, feeding me when I couldn't eat, comforting me when I was inconsolable, giving me time and space to heal and to write this book – I am so grateful to you. You and your family are our honorary Ukrainians, and my life would not be the same without you all.

Finally, thank you to the Ukrainian people, both in Ukraine, recently displaced and in our huge diaspora, those who I know and those who I do not. Thank you for your humanity, resilience and strength. This is my family story, but I hope that it may serve as a palimpsest of your own. I hope this book can be used to explain our collective struggle not through headlines, dates and lines on a map but through love and human emotions.

A Note on the Author

Olia Hercules was born in Kakhovka, in the south of Ukraine. She trained at the renowned Leiths School of Food and Wine, then worked as chef de partie in restaurants, including Ottolenghi, and as a recipe developer. Her first book, *Mamushka*, went on to win the Fortnum & Mason Award for best debut cookbook and was followed by *Kaukasis*, *Summer Kitchens* and *Home Food*. After the full-scale invasion of Ukraine in 2022, Olia co-founded a global initiative to raise money for Ukraine through cooking, #CookForUkraine, with her friend Alissa Timoshkina, which has raised over £2 million pounds to date. She lives with her husband, food writer and photographer Joe Woodhouse, and two sons in London.

A Note on the Type

The text of this book is set in Fournier. Fournier is derived from the *romain du roi*, which was created towards the end of the seventeenth century from designs made by a committee of the Académie of Sciences for the exclusive use of the Imprimerie Royale. The original Fournier types were cut by the famous Paris founder Pierre Simon Fournier in about 1742. These types were some of the most influential designs of the eight and are counted among the earliest examples of the 'transitional' style of typeface. This Monotype version dates from 1924. Fournier is a light, clear face whose distinctive features are capital letters that are quite tall and bold in relation to the lower-case letters, and *decorative italics, which show the influence of the calligraphy of Fournier's time.*

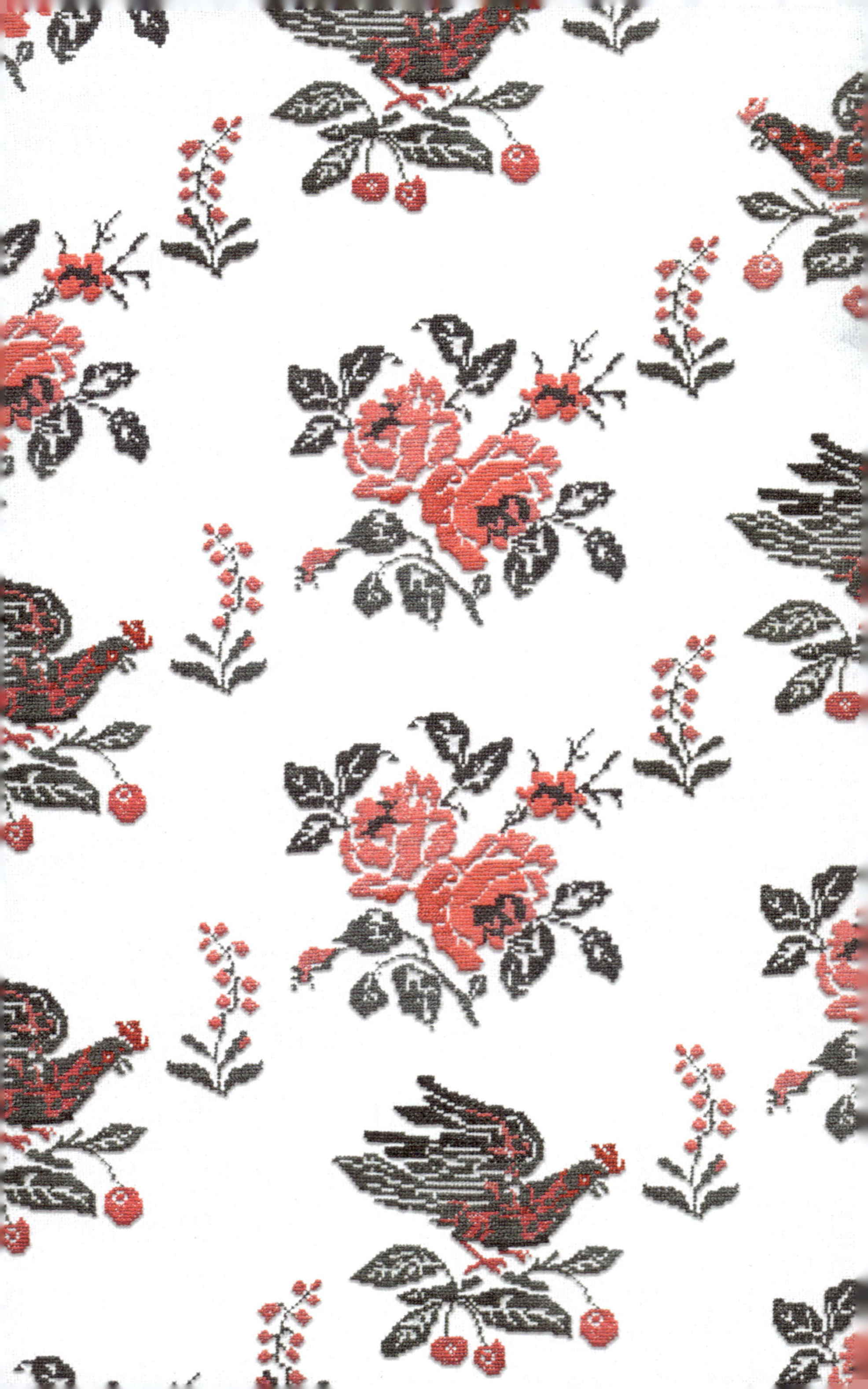